THE
POCKET
EDITION

Trivial Pursuit ™

Rock and Pop

THE AUTHORIZED GAME BOOK

GUINNESS BOOKS

Design: Clive Sutherland
Design concept and cover design: Craig Dodd

© Guinness Superlatives Ltd and Horn Abbot International Limited 19:
Published in Great Britain by Guinness Superlatives Ltd,
33 London Road, Enfield, Middlesex

Printed in Great Britain by The Bath Press Ltd, Avon

'Guinness' is a registered trade mark of Guinness Superlatives Ltd

Trivial Pursuit is a game and trademark owned and licensed by Horn
Abbot International Limited

British Library Cataloguing in Publication Data
Trivial Pursuit : pocket edition : rock and pop.
  1. Music, Popular (Songs, etc.) — Miscellanea
780'.42'076   ML3470

ISBN 0-85112-870-X

HORN ABBOT
INTERNATIONAL

TM

New from Guinness — **The Pocket Edition of Trivial Pursuit!** The slimline Pocket Edition has been specially designed so that trivia fans can carry with them more than 1000 tantalizing trivia questions wherever they go. Now you can play Trivial Pursuit in the car, waiting for a bus, on a train, even in the bath — you need never be bored again.

Each Pocket Edition is arranged in quizzes, with the answers at the back of the book for easy reference. And to make sure that there's something for everyone there are three other separate titles — **Genus, Sport** and **The Movies,** each containing hours of classic trivia challenge!

ROCK AND POP EDITION

This Rock and Pop Pocket Edition contains 54 quizzes divided into six categories. The categories are coded:

(WM)	Words and Music
(S)	Stars
(R)	Rock
(P)	Pop
(RPM)	Revs Per Minute
(MW)	Music World

(1) Who, according to this duo, does Jesus love more than she will know?

(2) What was the name of Ray Stevens' miniature queen of the blues?

(3) Who owned Bob Dylan's farm?

(4) Who did the Beatles say 'hey' to?

(5) Who did Bobbie Gentry sing an ode to in 1967?

(6) Who did the Beach Boys see when they went to a dance, looking for romance?

(7) Who were Cathy's clowns in 1960?

(8) Which baby gave Rod Stewart a hit?

9 Kid Creole admitted that he isn't her daddy — who is she?

10 Which girl's name is used to rhyme with the title of the song 'Memphis Tennessee'?

11 Which of Marilyn Monroe's husbands is mentioned by name in 'Mrs Robinson'?

12 Which lady's name gave the Bachelors the title for their only UK number one hit?

13 Who got married in the title of a 1959 Buddy Holly hit?

14 What was the name of Michael Jackson's rat?

15 Which all-girl group was Robert de Niro waiting for?

16 Whose mother did Dr Hook ring?

17 Who were Neil Diamond's 'cracklin'' and 'sweet' girls?

18 What was Police's first top twenty UK hit?

19 With whose army did Elvis Costello have a hit in 1979?

20 Who, according to this band, had a lovely daughter?

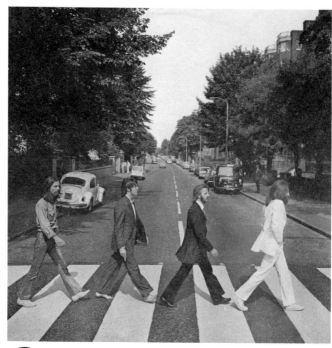

1 Which Beatles album had this cover?

2 Which is the most-recorded Beatles song?

3 Which Beatle had a solo hit with 'You're Sixteen'?

4 Who are the three grandchildren mentioned in the hit 'When I'm 64'?

5 What was the Beatles' biggest-selling single?

6 Which Liverpool nightclub first launched the Fab Four?

7 Which Beatle did *Private Eye* nickname Spiggy Topes?

8   What kind of Apple is on the Apple label?

9   Did Ringo play the drums on the American single release of 'Love Me Do'?

10   Which Beatles film features a mad scientist named Dr Foot?

11   Who managed the Beatles to stardom?

12   Which Beatles played themselves in the film *Give My Regards To Broad Street*?

13   Which Beatle was brought up by Aunt Mimi?

14   Who was the only Beatle to have had a full-time nine-to-five job?

15   Which folk singer allegedly gave the Beatles their first taste of 'grass' in August 1964?

16   What is Paul McCartney's first name?

17   Which Beatle was the first to become a grandad?

18   Which Beatles song opens, 'Last night I said these words to my girl'?

19   Which album originally contained the song 'Michelle'?

20   Who was the first Beatle to have a number one solo hit?

1 Who sang about her love of rock'n'roll in response to the Rolling Stones' 'It's Only Rock And Roll (But I Like It)'?

2 Who had a hit with 'It's Still Rock and Roll To Me'?

3 About whom did Julien Temple say, 'Their mission is to destroy rock and roll'?

4 Which American president used this rock poet's words in his inaugural speech?

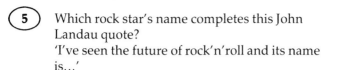

5 Which rock star's name completes this John Landau quote?
'I've seen the future of rock'n'roll and its name is…'

6 Who went to rock'n'roll high school?

7 Which band was rockin' all over the world at the Live Aid concert?

8 Who had a 1973 hit with 'Rock On'?

9 Who rocked the Casbah?

10 What, according to the Electric Light Orchestra's 1983 hit, is rock'n'roll?

11 Who was a 'Rock and Roll Suicide' in 1974?

12 Who had a hit with 'Rock And Roll (Parts 1 and 2)'?

13 Who had a thrilling hit with 'Rockin' Robin' in 1972?

14 Who had a 'Rock-A-Hula Baby'?

15 Which member of Queen called himself the Carmen Miranda of rock and roll?

16 Who had a 'Rock and Roll Heaven'?

17 Who had a hit with 'Nut Rocker'?

18 Who took 'I'm Just a Singer (In A Rock'n'Roll Band)' into the charts?

19 Who recorded 'Don't Knock The Rock'?

20 What kind of reptilian rock took Elton John into the top five?

1 With which hit-seeking group did Judith Durham find fame?

2 Which 1962 hit was named after an American communications satellite?

3 Who tiptoed through the tulips in 1968?

4 Which blind musician helped to launch Stevie Wonder's career?

5 Which Kinks song included the lines, 'I can't sail my yacht, The taxman's taken all I've got'?

6 Which album featured 'Eleanor Rigby' and 'Yellow Submarine'?

7 Who wrote the Monkees' hit 'I'm a Believer'?

8 Which father and daughter did 'Something Stupid' in 1967?

9 Which supergroup was once known as the Quarrymen?

10 Who had a 1964 hit with 'Um Um Um Um Um Um'?

11 To whom was Prince Philip referring when he told Canadians in 1965, 'They're on the wane'?

12 What kind of bikini gave Bryan Hyland his 1960 hit?

13 Who urged the world to do 'The Loco-motion'?

14 What was the Singing Nun's first and last hit?

15 What did Manfred Mann's girl say as she was walking down the street?

16 Who had a 1965 hit with 'Downtown'?

17 Which group was led by Freddie Garrity?

18 As what were Salvatore Phillip Bono and Cherilyn Sakisian La Pierre better known?

19 Which non-existent group had a hit with 'Sugar Sugar'?

20 With which song did this singer win the Eurovision Song Contest?

1 Which song was reputed to have netted Paul Simon more than $7 million in 1970?

2 Which pioneering soul singer had his first British success with 'You Send Me' in 1958?

3 Who had a hit with 'Papa's Got A Brand New Bag'?

4 Who was 'True Blue'in 1986?

5 From which of their albums did this band take their hit single 'Money for Nothing'?

6 Which heavy rock group scored their first and most successful hit with 'Black Night'?

7 Which 'young' group were 'Groovin'' in 1967?

8 Which Queen song was, at the time, the most expensive single ever to be recorded?

(9) 'Reach Out and Touch', in 1970, was the first solo effort by which Motown artist?

(10) Which group's greatest British success was 'Dedicated To The One I Love'?

(11) Who had a 1969 hit with 'Suspicious Minds'?

(12) Which month might it as well rain until according to Carole King's hit?

(13) Which comedy duo scored a posthumous hit in 1975 with 'The Trail Of The Lonesome Pine'?

(14) Who had a 1972 hit with 'Got To Be There'?

(15) Who had a solo success with 'I Only Have Eyes For You' and 'Bright Eyes'?

(16) Who were 'Pretty in Pink'?

(17) Who went for a walk on the wild side in 1973?

(18) Which of Crosby, Stills, Nash and Young went solo with 'Love The One You're With'?

(19) Which sparkling group of ladies hit the charts with 'Da Doo Ron Ron'?

(20) Which US group sliced out their only UK Top Ten hit with 'Make It With You'?

(1) Who wrote the title music for this film?

(2) Which movie produced the most US number one hits?

(3) Which Beatles movie featured the Blue Meanies?

(4) From which movie did Captain Sensible's hit 'Happy Talk' come?

(5) Which film had as its theme song 'Eye of the Tiger'?

(6) Which movie gave Lee Marvin a surprise hit with 'Wand'rin' Star'?

(7) Which American singer and songwriter made his film debut in *Cisco Pike*?

(8) Which Beatles film had the working titles *Beatlemania* and *What Little Old Man*?

(9) Which performer had a hit with the title song from *Fame*?

10 Which song from *An Officer and a Gentleman* won an Oscar?

11 Who wrote the title song for *9 to 5*?

12 Who did Diana Ross portray in *Lady Sings the Blues*?

13 Which singer received accolades for her performance in *Mask*?

14 To whom did David Bowie say 'Merry Christmas'?

15 Which folk rock star appeared in *Pat Garrett and Billy the Kid*?

16 Who starred with James Fox and Anita Pallenberg in *Performance*?

17 Which film followed Bill Haley's first big screen appearance in *Rock Around the Clock*?

18 What was the title of the movie that starred Abba?

19 Which late-night film had the theme song 'Everybody's Talking'?

20 In which movie did this singer make his first acting appearance?

(1) Which place is so good that 'they named it twice', according to Gerard Kenny's hit song?

(2) Which country cried for Julie Covington?

(3) Where did Wings 'always desire to be' in their 1979 mega-hit?

(4) Which city did this singer call 'my kind of town'?

(5) Where was the House of the Rising Sun?

6. Where, according to the Bee Gees, did the lights all go out?

7. Which city did Jimmy Osmond's long-haired lover hail from?

8. Where might Simon and Garfunkel have been able to buy parsley, sage, rosemary and thyme?

9. Where did the girl in Astrid Gilberto's most famous song come from?

10. Where did the Monkees go on the last train?

11. Where did Supertramp have their hit breakfast?

12. What did the Beach Boys wish all girls could be?

13. Where did Bonnie Tyler get lost for her first hit?

14. Where did David Bowie's 1983 hit girl come from?

15. Which state does John Denver call his mountain Momma?

16. What did Ray Charles have on his mind?

17. Where was Daniel 'travelling tonight on a plane' according to Elton John?

18. Where was Sweet Marie waiting for Tony Orlando?

19. Which city did Ralph McTell offer to show you?

20. What, according to Perry Como, did Delaware?

1 Which pop star bought the publishing rights to Buddy Holly's songs?

2 What, according to the experts, was Jackie Brenston's 'Rocket 88'?

3 The rock music of which artist was featured on a recording launched into space in 1977 aboard Voyagers 1 and 2 — Buddy Holly, Bill Haley or Chuck Berry?

4 Who wrote and had a first-time hit with 'Be-Bop-A-Lula'?

5 What, according to Eddie Cochran, ain't there no cure for?

6 Why did Don McLean refer to 3 February 1959 as 'the day the music died'?

7 Which early guitar hero was famed for his triangular, star-shaped and fur-covered guitars?

8 Which pianist was known as The Fat Man?

9 What were the Christian names of the Everly Brothers?

10 Who wrote 'Memphis Tennessee'?

11 Which rocker left Britain after admitting he had married his 13-year-old second cousin?

12 Which future pop star was the first policeman to arrive at the scene of the accident which killed Eddie Cochran?

13 To whom did Little Richard say 'Good Golly'?

14 Which British band was named in Buddy Holly's memory?

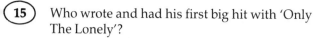

15 Who wrote and had his first big hit with 'Only The Lonely'?

16 Who did early rocker Shane Fenton become in later life?

17 Which middle-aged rock and roll pioneer had a kiss curl as his trademark?

18 What was Buddy Holly's posthumous number one?

19 Who was known as the Wild Man of Rock'n'Roll?

20 Who is this pioneer of soul and rock and roll?

(1) Which ex-glitter band is shown here?

(2) With what name did Queen start out — Sunshine, Smile or the Happy Faces?

(3) The music of which artist was described as 'Rock'n'roll with lipstick on'?

(4) Which glittering star started life as Paul Raven and nearly became Terry Tinsel?

(5) About which band did Ringo Starr make the film *Born To Boogie*?

(6) Who sang about Lady Marmalade while wearing lamé space suits?

(7) Which glitter rocker changed his name to avoid confusion with Davy Jones of the Monkees?

(8) Which American band wears so much make-up that they boast that their faces are unknown to their fans?

(9) Which 'sugary' British band had a hit with 'Love Is Like Oxygen'?

(10) Which band had UK number ones with 'Rivers of Babylon' and 'Mary's Boy Child'?

(11) Which star wore one glittering glove for a thrilling success?

(12) Who had his first UK number one with 'I'm The Leader of The Gang (I Am)'?

(13) Which glam-rock singer acknowledges the influence of Liza Minelli in his performance?

(14) Which group featured in a comic book whose red ink supposedly contained blood from the band members?

(15) With which band did Peter Gabriel appear dressed as a flower?

(16) Who dressed up for the 'Y. M. C. A.' in 1979?

(17) Who wrote the glitter anthem 'All The Young Dudes' for Mott the Hoople?

(18) With which band did David Bowie have the hit 'Under Pressure'?

(19) Which fancy-dress band was made up of 'Marco, Merrick, Terry Lee, Gary Tibbs and yours truly'?

(20) What is this glitter star's real name?

1 Which song gave Rolf Harris a hit in 1970?

2 Who did Father Abraham team up with for three 1978 hits?

3 What did Lynn Anderson promise in 1970?

4 Who promised 'You Ain't Seen Nothin' Yet' in 1974?

5 Who took 'Can't Get Enough' into the charts?

6 Who had a 1972 hit with 'Me And Julio Down By The Schoolyard'?

7 Who was Thin Lizzie's late lamented lead singer?

8 Who shot up the charts with 'Rubber Bullets'?

9 What was the real-life relationship between Shirley Jones and David Cassidy of *The Partridge Family*?

10 Did Smokey Robinson write the words or the music of 'The Tears of a Clown'?

11 With which Carole King record did James Taylor achieve his biggest hit in 1971?

12 Who had a brand new pair of roller skates and a hit with a 'Brand New Key'?

13 Which film made 'The First Time Ever I Saw Your Face' a hit in 1972?

14 Who made his debut dressed as a clown and singing 'The Show Must Go On'?

15 Who assured us 'I Am Woman'?

(16) Which Judy Collins hit went in and out of the UK Top Fifty on eight occasions between 1970 and 1972?

(17) Which group ended a string of 21 Top Twenty hits with 'The Air That I Breathe'?

(18) Which American band had a 1970 UK hit with 'Let's Work Together'?

(19) What, in 1979, became Pink Floyd's first UK number one hit single?

(20) At which number on Ocean Boulevard did this artist live?

▼

(1) What was this singer's first solo Top Three hit?

(2) Which lengthy Beatles single was the first released on their Apple label?

(3) Who sang about the morning DJ on W. O. L. D. in 1974?

(4) What street was Bob Dylan positively on?

(5) Which duo made it into the charts with 'Yesterday Once More'?

6 Who sang about 'Lady D'Arbanville' in 1970?

7 Which duo had hits with 'Only You' and 'Nobody's Diary' before going their separate ways?

8 Who created a catchphrase with his 1956 hit 'See You Later Alligator'?

9 Which three methods of transport carried Billy J. Kramer and the Dakotas into the charts in 1965?

10 What day of the week gave the Mamas and the Papas a hit?

11 Who led his group up the charts with 'Lady Willpower'?

12 Who had her first hit with 'Kids in America'?

13 Who sang about 'Misstra Know It All'?

14 Which Beatle provided lead vocals for 'With a Little Help From My Friends'?

15 Who was trying to 'Catch The Wind'?

16 Which Don McLean song had a playing time of eight minutes and twenty-seven seconds?

17 Which Moroccan train did Crosby, Stills and Nash immortalize in song?

18 Which song by the Troggs was also recorded by Jimi Hendrix?

19 Who followed 'Walk Right Back' with 'Temptation'?

20 Which Rolling Stones hit was written about David Bowie's wife Angela?

1 Which married couple had a 1974 hit with 'Mockingbird'?

2 Which folk-influenced duo had their first hit with 'The Sounds of Silence'?

3 Under what name did folksy duo Peter Asher and Gordon Waller perform?

4 What kind of transport took Joni Mitchell up the charts?

5 In which popular folk group did Mary Travers sing?

6 After which poet did Robert Zimmerman name himself?

7 Which folk-pop band had a hit with 'California Dreamin''?

8 What was the title of Ralph McTell's 1974 hit?

9 Which folk rocker was a Sunshine Superman?

10 Who wrote and had a hit with 'What Have They Done To My Song, Ma'?

11 Who took 'Lay Lady Lay' into the charts?

12 Which rock star sang backing vocals on Carly Simon's 'You're So Vain'?

13 Who wrote the folk standard 'Where Have All The Flowers Gone'?

14 Who looked at life from 'Both Sides Now'?

15 Which Beatle co-wrote 'If Not For You' with Bob Dylan?

16 Who recorded the albums *Blood On The Tracks* and *Desire*?

17 Which Australian folk-pop group scored an international hit with 'I'll never Find Another You'?

18 Which folk trio took 'Blowin' in the Wind' into the charts?

19 What, in 1975, did Judy Collins ask us to send in?

20 With whom did this singer have the relationship that provided the subject material for her hit 'Diamonds and Rust'?

1 Who lived her life like a candle in the wind, according to Elton John?

2 Who had his own song, 'Jealous Guy', released by Roxy Music as a tribute after his death?

3 Who is the real-life Jude of 'Hey Jude'?

4 Who did Carly Simon allegedly have in mind when she wrote 'You're So Vain'?

5 Which Don McLean song laments the day this man died?

▼

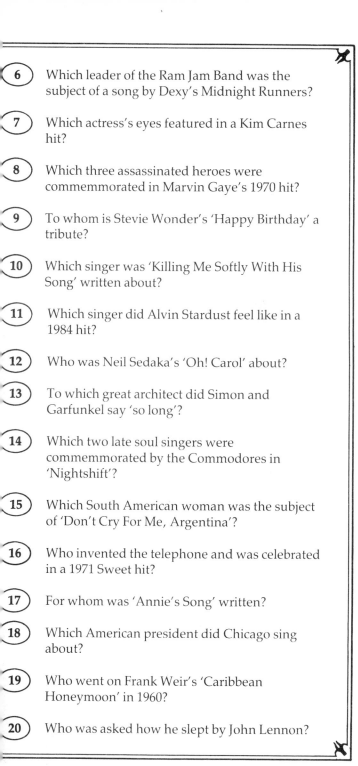

6) Which leader of the Ram Jam Band was the subject of a song by Dexy's Midnight Runners?

7) Which actress's eyes featured in a Kim Carnes hit?

8) Which three assassinated heroes were commemmorated in Marvin Gaye's 1970 hit?

9) To whom is Stevie Wonder's 'Happy Birthday' a tribute?

10) Which singer was 'Killing Me Softly With His Song' written about?

11) Which singer did Alvin Stardust feel like in a 1984 hit?

12) Who was Neil Sedaka's 'Oh! Carol' about?

13) To which great architect did Simon and Garfunkel say 'so long'?

14) Which two late soul singers were commemmorated by the Commodores in 'Nightshift'?

15) Which South American woman was the subject of 'Don't Cry For Me, Argentina'?

16) Who invented the telephone and was celebrated in a 1971 Sweet hit?

17) For whom was 'Annie's Song' written?

18) Which American president did Chicago sing about?

19) Who went on Frank Weir's 'Caribbean Honeymoon' in 1960?

20) Who was asked how he slept by John Lennon?

(1) Who was the drummer who was asked to leave this band?

(2) Which band backs Ian Dury?

(3) Who was backed by Cockney Rebel?

(4) Who was Smokey Robinson's most frequent backing group?

(5) Which female rocker fronts the Blackhearts?

(6) Who was the driving force behind the Silver Bullet Band?

(7) Which band backed Billy J. Kramer?

(8) Who is married to one of his own Coconuts?

9 Who headed the MGs?

10 Which band was founded by Demis Roussos and Vangelis?

11 Who did the Band most famously back?

12 Whose Bluesbreakers included Eric Clapton, John McVie and Mick Taylor?

13 Which band is led by Midge Ure?

14 Which group did the Alan Price Combo become?

15 Which group backed up Frankie Lymon?

16 Who was backed by the Vandellas?

17 To what did Tyrannosaurus Rex change their name in 1970?

18 Who was backed by the Mothers of Invention?

19 Which band emerged as the result of an advert which read, 'Wanted: four insane boys, aged 17-21, to form a group for a TV show'?

20 Who paced behind Gerry in the sixties?

(1) How much were Alice Cooper's 'babies' worth in 1973?

(2) Which British heavy metal band is named after a medieval torture device?

(3) Which band had a hit single with 'Smoke on the Water'?

(4) Which author coined the term 'heavy metal' in his novel *Naked Lunch*?

(5) To which band, led by Francis Rossi and Rick Parfitt, did the Princess of Wales tap her foot at the Live Aid concert?

(6) Who recorded the soundtrack of the movie *Deathwish II*?

(7) Which band did Ian Gillan leave to pursue a solo career?

(8) Who left King Crimson to join Emerson and Palmer?

(9) Which heavy rock band has replaced the Zombies to come last in alphabetical lists of chart successes?

(10) Which heavy metal singer became notorious after biting off the head of a live bat on stage?

(11) Which heavy metal band started out as the New Yardbirds?

(12) Dusty Hill, Frank Beard and Billy Gibbons make up which band?

(13) Which band was led by Robert Fripp?

(14) Who were *Screaming for Vengeance* on the album charts in 1982?

15 Which band is this?

16 Which member of Led Zeppelin owns the former house of satanist Aleister Crowley?

17 Who was lead singer with Black Sabbath before pursuing a solo career?

18 AC/DC hail from which country?

19 Which heavy metal band named itself after a Hermann Hesse novel?

20 Who is lead singer with Van Halen?

1 Which of this star's hits began, 'Warden threw a party in the county jail'?

2 Which Monkees hit included the words, 'Cheer up sleepy Jean, Oh what can it mean'?

3 Which song began, 'There's nothing you can do that can't be done'?

4 Which of Carole King's hits starts, 'When you're down and troubled and you need someone to care'?

5 Who asked the musical question, 'Do Ya Think I'm Sexy'?

6 Which Seekers song went, 'There's a new world somewhere, for each of us they say'?

7. Which song begins, 'If there's anything that you want'?

8. In which of his hits did Frank Sinatra 'dooby dooby doo'?

9. Which song contains the line, 'I'm sitting in a railway station, Got a ticket for my destination'?

10. Which song begins, 'Little darlin', it's been a long, cold, lonely winter'?

11. Which 1965 song had the line, 'Like taking candy from a baby'?

12. Which song begins, 'Once upon a time there was a tavern'?

13. Which Beatles song contains the words, 'The girl that's driving me mad is going away'?

14. Which song opens with the line, 'Tonight you're mine completely'?

15. Which Sonny and Cher hit went, 'Then put your little hand in mine, There ain't no hill or mountain we can't climb'?

16. Which song begins, 'Wise men say, Only fools rush in'?

17. Which of the Beach Boys' hits includes, 'My buddies and me are getting real well known'?

18. Which song goes, 'I did what I had to do, And saw it through without exemption'?

19. Which Cat Stevens song includes the line, 'A cup of cold coffee and a piece of cake'?

20. What was the colour of Donovan's 'true love's hair' in the song 'Colours'?

1 Which group hit it big with 'Jive Talkin'' in 1975?

2 Who had a 1964 hit with 'When A Man Loves A Woman'?

3 Who scored with 'A Boy Named Sue'?

4 Which song gave Jackie Wilson a UK hit in 1957 and 1986?

5 Who clawed his way to a 1977 success with 'The Year of the Cat'?

6 Which two stars got together to record 'The Girl Is Mine' in 1982?

7 Which group had a huge sixties hit with 'Where Did Our Love Go'?

8 Which duo insisted 'She Means Nothing To Me' in 1983?

9 Whose last chart topper was 'Mighty Quinn' in 1968?

10 Who took 'Lady in Red' to a UK number one in 1986?

11 Which vocal group had a hit with 'Then He Kissed Me' in 1963?

12 What advice did Ray Charles offer Jack?

13 Who posed the lyrical question 'Do You Know The Way To San Jose'?

14 Which late American songwriter wrote the Rolling Stones hit 'Not Fade Away'?

15 Who concluded 'I Guess That's Why They Call It The Blues'?

16 What was on the flip side of the 'Penny Lane' single?

17 Which Motown group joined Diana Ross and the Supremes on 'I'm Gonna Make You Love Me'?

18 Which group's biggest hit was 'Be My Baby'?

19 Which rock and roll classic became a hit after featuring in the film *The Blackboard Jungle*?

20 What was this band's first and most controversial hit?

1 Which songstress had a hit with 'My Guy' in 1964?

2 Who founded the Motown label?

3 Whose 'Shop Around' was the first miraculous million-seller for Motown?

4 Who had his first US number one with the live single 'Fingertips (Pt. II)'?

5 Who did Billy Preston pair up with for the 1980 hit 'With You I'm Born Again'?

6 Who is this artist who heard it through the grapevine for a hit in 1968?

7 In which 'motortown' was Motown established?

8 Which all-girl group started out as the Primettes?

9 Who had a 1982 hit with the Supremes' 'You Can't Hurry Love'?

10 Who was the main songwriter for the Commodores before he left to go solo?

11 Which group had a 1971 hit with 'Just My Imagination (Running Away With Me)'?

12 Which group featured members called Toriano, Sigmund, Jermaine, Marlon and Michael?

13 In which year was Marvin Gaye killed?

14 For which film was Stevie Wonder's hit 'I Just Called To Say I Loved You' written?

15 Who had a 1970 hit with 'The Tears of a Clown'?

16 Which Motown group, comprising Levi Stubbs, Abdul Fakir, Lawrence Payton and Renaldo Benson have been recording together for more than thirty years?

17 Which Tamla Motown star was born Steveland Morris?

18 After which Debbie Reynolds hit did Berry Gordy name his Tamla record label?

19 Which Four Tops song had 'Sugar Pie, Honey Bunch' in brackets after the title?

20 Which Motown artist was banned in South Africa after accepting his Oscar on behalf of Nelson Mandela?

(1) Which year in the future took Zager and Evans to the top?

(2) How many hours from Tulsa was Gene Pitney?

(3) What kind of working day was shared by Dolly Parton and Sheena Easton?

(4) How many ways are there to leave your lover, according to Paul Simon?

(5) Which crash landed Suzi Quatro in the charts?

(6) How many tons took Tennessee Ernie Ford to the top?

(7) How many little birds did Bob Marley sing about?

(8) How many tribes went to Frankie's war?

(9) What number was the Electric Light Orchestra's 1972 Overture?

(10) What kind of pack did Police release in 1980?

(11) How many steps did Eddie Cochran take to heaven?

(12) Which nervous breakdown did the Rolling Stones experience in 1966?

(13) How many broken hearts did Elvis Presley have for sale?

(14) How many miles high did the Byrds fly?

(15) What time was the train that took the Who up the charts?

(16) On which bridge did Simon and Garfunkel feel groovy?

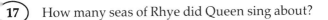

17 How many seas of Rhye did Queen sing about?

18 How many red balloons did Nena have?

19 What was the average age of American soldiers in Vietnam, according to Paul Hardcastle?

20 What number links George Orwell with this duo's 'Sexcrime'?

1 What was this guitarist's 'royal' nickname?

2 Which Moody Blues guitarist joined Wings?

3 Who left Deep Purple in 1975 to take on his own Rainbow?

4 Which guitarist of the fifties and sixties was named after a one-stringed African guitar?

5 Which of Crosby, Stills, Nash and Young had played with the Hollies?

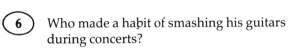

6 Who made a habit of smashing his guitars during concerts?

7 Which British instrumental group had a 1962 hit with 'Guitar Tango'?

8 In which band does Joe Strummer play?

9 Which guitarist formed Derek and the Dominoes?

10 Which of the Allman Brothers appears with Eric Clapton on 'Layla' — Duane or Gregg?

11 Which guitarist took over from Pink Floyd's Syd Barrett in 1968?

12 Which guitar man swapped the Yardbirds for Cream?

13 Who played lead guitar for the Who?

14 Who set fire to his guitar for the first time at Finsbury Park, London on 31 March 1967?

15 In which area of science does Queen guitarist Brian May have a Ph.D?

16 Which heavy rock guitarist played on Michael Jackson's 'Beat It'?

17 Who was the Free guitarist who died of a drugs overdose in 1976?

18 Which great guitarist started out leading a band called Jimmy James and the Blue Flames?

19 Which Faces guitarist suffers from multiple sclerosis?

20 Who was Led Zeppelin's lead guitarist?

1 Who played with Curved Air before joining Police?

2 Who had their first hit with 'Once In A Lifetime' in 1981?

3 Which new wave duo are named after a Greek term describing graceful and harmonious rhythm?

4 Which band has a lead singer called Bono Vox?

5 Which Blondie hit featured in *American Gigolo*?

6 Who was *Born To Run*?

7 Which band recorded *Zenyatta Mondatta*?

8 Which of his characters, stranded in 'Space Oddity' in 1969, did David Bowie revive in 'Ashes to Ashes'?

9 Which two brothers founded Dire Straits?

10 Who didn't have to give 'Tainted Love' a hard sell?

11 Which Downtown Boy married his 'Uptown Girl'?

12 On which philosopher's work did Police base their album *Synchronicity*?

13 Which female singer caused a stir by turning up to a Grammy ceremony dressed as Elvis Presley?

14 Which of his songs, according to Sting, is about 'surveillance and ownership and jealousy'?

15 Who is Nils Lofgren's boss?

16 Who sang for the Jam before moving on to found his own Style Council?

17 On which Dire Straits album is Sting billed as appearing?

18 Which philanthropic rocker has a daughter named Fifi Trixibelle?

19 Which rock star appeared in commercials for Wrigleys gum and Triumph bras?

20 From which of this star's films did 'When Doves Cry' come?

(1) Which Paul Simon album is named after Elvis Presley's home?

(2) In response to which of the Beatles' albums did the Rolling Stones record *Their Satanic Majesties Request*?

(3) *Can't Slow Down* was voted best LP of 1984 — who recorded it?

(4) What kind of animal sits on Michael Jackson's knee inside the cover of the *Thriller* album?

(5) What was this band's most successful album?

(6) What was controversial about John Lennon and Yoko Ono's *Two Virgins* album?

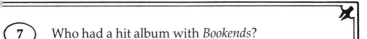

(7) Who had a hit album with *Bookends*?

(8) Which band welcomed us to the Pleasure Dome?

(9) Which artist had a 1974 album called *Caribou*?

(10) What is written in flowers beneath the group photograph on the *Sgt. Pepper* album sleeve?

(11) What is the title of Pink Floyd's most successful album?

(12) Who discovered that you don't require a jacket to have a hit album?

(13) What was the title of Bob Dylan's 1968 album — *Jean Paul Sartre*, *John Wesley Harding* or *Thomas Wesley Hardy*?

(14) Who took *Never A Dull Moment* into the charts in 1972?

(15) The album *Sweet Baby James* was recorded by which folk singer?

(16) Which album is reputed to have made the Who millionaires?

(17) Which Zeppelin appeared on the cover of Led Zeppelin's first album?

(18) Who won five Grammy awards in 1974 for the album *Innervisions*?

(19) Which duo released *The Final* before splitting up?

(20) Who *Let It Bleed* in 1969?

(1) Who joined Diana Ross in 'Stop Look Listen (To Your Heart)'?

(2) Who sang 'Happy Birthday Sweet Sixteen' in 1961?

(3) Which American group galloped up the charts with 'Horse With No Name'?

(4) On which novel by Emily Bronte did Kate Bush base her first hit?

(5) What was the name of the girl who gave Dion the runaround in 1961?

(6) With which Doors song did Jose Feliciano win a Grammy award?

(7) Which Beatles song was a 1966 hit for David and Jonathan?

(8) Who had her first, and so far only, number one with 'Ring My Bell'?

(9) Who provided the heavy breathing at the end of Rod Stewart's 'Tonight's The Night'?

(10) Who had a hit with 'Sweet Caroline' in 1971?

(11) Which Phil Spector-produced group had a hit with 'Baby I Love You'?

(12) Who vowed 'I Will Survive' in 1979?

(13) Which group had a 1966 hit with 'God Only Knows'?

(14) What was the title of Elvis's hit version of 'O Sole Mio'?

(15) Who was a 'Material Girl' in 1985?

16 What was this singer gonna tear down in 1984?

17 Which Bob Dylan song put the Byrds on their perch?

18 Who had a 1984 hit with 'Let's Hear It For The Boy'?

19 Who had a big, *big* hit with 'It's Raining Men'?

20 Which miraculous song did Culture Club sing in 1984?

(1) What was this disco queen's first chart hit?

(2) Which song took German disco artist Patrick Hernandez into the charts in 1979?

(3) Who urged the world to do 'Le Freak'?

(4) Which disco film was based on a feature entitled 'Tribal Rights of the New Saturday Night' in *New York* magazine?

(5) Which 'disco' song took Johnny Taylor into the charts in 1976?

(6) With whom did Donna Summer record 'No More Tears (Enough Is Enough)'?

7 Which 1983 hit movie gave Irene Cara chart success and sent breakdancing popularity soaring?

8 Who took 'We Are Family' into the dance charts?

9 Who was crowned Queen of the Discos by the National Association of Discotheque Disc Jockeys in 1975?

10 Who suggested 'Let's Dance' for a 1983 number one?

11 Which Donna Summer hit had been a success for Richard Harris ten years earlier?

12 What nationality is disco producer Giorgio Moroder?

13 Who hit it big with a disco version of 'Never Can Say Goodbye' in 1974?

14 What did Amii Stewart knock in 1979?

15 Who had their first number one with the disco-orientated 'Heart Of Glass'?

16 Which disco star once sang with the Vienna Folk Opera?

17 Who had a 'Disco Inferno'?

18 Which band had a shining dance hit with 'That's The Way (I Like It)'?

19 Who wrote 'Dancing In The Dark'?

20 With which band did Nile Rogers make his disco name?

1 Who wrote Lionel Richie's hit 'All Night Long'?

2 Who wrote Peter and Gordon's 1964 hit 'A World Without Love'?

3 Which of the Beach Boys wrote 'I Get Around'?

4 Who wrote and sang the theme song for *Absolute Beginners*?

5 Who wrote the lyrics to Elton John's early hits?

6 Which is the most frequently sung song in England?

7 Who wrote 'Careless Whisper'?

8 Which US folk singer wrote 'If I Had A Hammer'?

9 Which Ed Cobb song gave Soft Cell a 1981 hit?

10 Who writes most of Dire Straits' material?

11 Who wrote and had a hit with 'Like To Get To Know You Well'?

12 Which best-selling Christmas record was written by Irving Berlin?

13 Which member of the Bee Gees wrote the theme song for the film *Grease* — Andy, Barry or Robin?

14 Which star of the silent screen wrote 'This Is My Song', a 1967 hit for Petula Clark?

15 Which two pop stars wrote 'We Are The World' for USA For Africa?

16 Who wrote the Kinks' 'You Really Got Me'?

(17) Who wrote 'I Don't LIke Mondays' for the Boomtown Rats?

(18) Who wrote the music for Julio Iglesias's hit 'Begin The Beguine'?

(19) Which duo wrote 'Jailhouse Rock'?

(20) Who wrote this band's prudent 1983 hit?

(1) Who is this Rolling Stone and what instrument does he play?

(2) What was the Rolling Stones' first UK number one?

(3) Which Rolling Stone said, 'I give the impression of being bored, but I'm not really. I've just got an incredibly boring face'?

(4) Who wrote the Stones' second single 'I Wanna Be Your Man'?

(5) From which album were 'Sympathy For The Devil' and 'Street Fighting Man' taken?

(6) Which Stones' song is about the Boston Strangler?

(7) What nationality was Mick Jagger's first wife, Bianca?

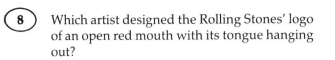

(8) Which artist designed the Rolling Stones' logo of an open red mouth with its tongue hanging out?

(9) Which Rolling Stone said, 'I have the rare distinction of being the only person so far to have left the Rolling Stones and lived'?

(10) Which precious stone did Mick Jagger first have implanted in one of his front teeth?

(11) Which of the Stones has a child called Dandelion?

(12) Which Stone lived and died on the former estate of Winnie-the-Pooh's creator, A. A. Milne?

(13) Who directed the film *Performance*, in which Mick Jagger starred?

(14) Which of the Stones released the solo album *Monkey Grip*?

(15) At which Rolling Stones concert was a man in the audience killed by Hell's Angels?

(16) Which of Mick Jagger's girlfriends had a hit with 'As Tears Go By'?

(17) What kind of creatures did Mick Jagger set free at the Hyde Park Festival in memory of Brian Jones?

(18) Who did Mick Jagger perform live with at the Live Aid concert?

(19) What runs up and down on the *Sticky Fingers* album?

(20) Which of the Rolling Stones attended the London School of Economics?

1 Which instrument is played by Ike Turner?

2 Who is Status Quo's drummer?

3 What instrument is played by Jerry Dammers of the Specials fame?

4 In which band did Brian Eno make his name playing synthesizer?

5 Who played bass for Thin Lizzie?

6 What instrument does Stray Cat Slim Jim play?

7 In which band does John McVie play bass guitar?

8 Who replaced Keith Moon as drummer of the Who?

9 Which instrument does Andy MacKay play?

10 Who taught George Harrison to play the sitar?

11 Who played sitar and dulcimer with the Rolling Stones?

12 What is synthesizer player Evangelous Papathanassiou better known as?

13 Who is the drummer with Culture Club?

14 In which band does John Entwhistle play bass?

15 Which piano-player was promoted as the '12-year-old genius'?

16 Who played the drums in the Carpenters?

17 In which band does Jean-Jacques Burnel play bass?

18 What instrument is played by Cozy Powell?

19 Which keyboard player left Yes to pursue a solo career?

A   B   C

20 Who is the lead guitarist in this group — A, B or C?

(1) With which song did this pair have a 1983 US number one?

(2) Don McLean's song 'Vincent' describes which painter?

(3) What was Police's first UK number one?

(4) Who walked back to happiness for a number one hit in 1961?

(5) What, according to Sheb Wooley's US number one hit, is purple, has one eye, one horn and eats people?

(6) Which band had a US number one with 'Centerfold'?

(7) Who shared the credit for 'Je T'Aime… Moi Non Plus' with Jane Birkin?

(8) The proceeds from which Rod Stewart number one were donated to UNICEF?

(9) Who put time in a bottle for a posthumous 1973 US number one?

(10) Who took the midnight train to Georgia in 1973?

(11) What did Dawn's ex-convict ask his wife to do if she wanted him back?

(12) Which bird took Fleetwood Mac to number one?

(13) Which song was number one in the UK for Christmas 1984?

(14) His ding-a-ling was banned but went to the top anyway in 1972 — who is he?

(15) Who had a UK number one with 'Where Do You Go To My Lovely'?

(16) What is the full title of the Rolling Stones song 'Satisfaction'?

(17) Which John Lennon song took over five years to get to number one in the UK?

(18) Which Lionel Richie and Diana Ross song is said to be the most successful duet of all time?

(19) Who composed the *Chariots of Fire* theme?

(20) Which band didn't have a tragedy when 'Tragedy' went to number one?

1 Which baldy talked his way into the charts with 'If'?

2 Which group scored their one and only British number one with 'That'll Be The Day' in 1957?

3 What did the Four Tops advise Renee to do?

4 Which festival provided a number one for Matthew's Southern Comfort?

5 Who sang with the Electric Light Orchestra on 'Xanadu'?

6 Which film provided the number one hit 'Summer Nights'?

7 Who, with his Gang, took 'Joanna' into the charts in 1984?

8 Which Liverpool group of the eighties saw its first three singles go to number one in the UK charts?

9 Who had a hit with the Bee Gees song 'Woman In Love'?

10 Whose first hit song was 'It's Not Unusual'?

11 Which young heart-throb had a chart hit with 'How Can I Be Sure'?

12 Which group made it into the charts with 'I Want To Know What Love Is'?

13 Which 1965 Temptations hit was recorded in response to Mary Wells' 'My Guy'?

14 What night of the week was 'all right for fighting' according to Elton John?

15 Who partnered this singer to success with 'Easy Lover'?

16 Which brothers had hits with 'Behind A Painted Smile' and 'Summer Breeze'?

17 Which group climbed the charts in 1984 with 'I Want To Break Free'?

18 Which Marvin Gaye song was revived for Paul Young's first UK hit?

19 For which band was 'Every Little Thing She Does Is Magic' magic?

20 Who duetted with Willie Nelson on 'To All The Girls I've Loved Before'?

1 Who leads the Maytals?

2 Which British reggae-inspired group is sometimes known as the Camden Nutty Boys?

3 With which song did the Piglets have a 1971 UK hit?

4 Which religion has had a strong influence on ska and reggae music and musicians?

5 Which band backed this reggae star?

6. Who had a hit with 'Israelites'?

7. What kind of soldier did Bob Marley take into the UK charts in 1983?

8. Who had a hit with 'Wonderful World, Beautiful People'?

9. Which 'black' band's title is based on the Swahili for freedom?

10. Who used a reggae beat for his hit song 'Mother and Child Reunion'?

11. Who had a backing band called the Aces?

12. On which island is Bob Marley buried?

13. Which band had a reggae-inspired hit with 'The Tide Is High'?

14. Who covered John Denver's 'Country Roads', changing 'West Virginia' to 'West Jamaica'?

15. Who took Bob Marley's 'I Shot The Sheriff' up the charts?

16. Who had their one and only UK number one with 'Up Town Top Ranking'?

17. Who took Al Capone into the charts?

18. Which reggae star was backed by a female vocal trio called the I-Threes?

19. Who had a hit with 'I Can See Clearly Now'?

20. Which British reggae band is named after an unemployment benefit card?

1 What words are missing from the title of this Lonnie Donegan hit — 'Does Your — — Lose It's Flavour?'

2 What did Stevie Wonder call to say to achieve his first UK number one?

3 Which James Taylor song contains the line, 'I seen sunny days that I thought would never end'?

4 What was Doris Day's mother's Spanish reply when Doris asked 'What will I be?'

5 What preceded 'Park' in the title of a Small Faces 1967 hit?

6 What were Dire Straits 'Sultans of'?

7 Which song begins, 'When I find myself in times of trouble'?

8 Which Shangri-Las hit starts with the question, 'Is she really going out with him?'

9 Which of the Who's songs includes the line, 'I was born with a plastic spoon in my mouth'?

10 Which song includes the line, 'Sont les mots qui vont tres bien ensemble'?

11 What shouldn't you step on even if you, 'Burn my house, steal my car, drink my liquor from an old fruit jar'?

12 Which Elton John song includes the line, 'She packed my bags last night pre-flight'?

13 In which song did Cliff Richard sing, 'We're going where the sun shines brightly. We're going where the sea is blue'?

14 Which of this singer's songs went, 'And if I ever lose my legs, I won't moan and I won't beg'?

15 Which Elton John song contains the line, 'All the papers had to say, was that Marilyn was found in the nude'?

16 Who noted that, 'Short people got no reason to live'?

17 What was in the sandwich in the 1983 hit 'Down Under'?

18 Who 'took the last train for the coast' in 'American Pie'?

19 Which Beatles song features John Lennon singing, 'You're gonna crucify me'?

20 Which Peter, Paul and Mary song contains the line, 'So kiss me and smile for me'?

(1) What was this star's nickname?

(2) Who took time off from rock to play Mabel in *The Pirates of Penzance*?

(3) Who is lead singer with Fleetwood Mac?

(4) Who partners Dave Stewart to form Eurythmics?

(5) Who accompanied Florence Ballard and Mary Wilson to nine consecutive hits?

(6) Who was the Velvet Underground's female drummer?

(7) Who was backed by Big Brother and the Holding Company and the Full Tilt Boogie Band?

(8) Which famous blonde played a brunette in *Union City*?

(9) Who heard 'Thunder In The Mountains' before packing them in as Trafford Tanzi and appearing opposite Laurence Olivier?

(10) With which underground band did Nico make her name?

11 What was Bonnie Tyler holding out for?

12 Who graced Jefferson Airplane before boarding Jefferson Starship?

13 Who was presented with a fur coat by the distillers of Southern Comfort for her sterling work in publicizing the brew?

14 Who shared the cover of *Time* with Governor Jerry Brown?

15 Who was born Annie Mae Bullock in Brownsville, Tennessee in 1938?

16 Who enjoyed *Happy Days* on screen after a hit with 'Devil Gate Drive'?

17 Which protest singer of the sixties founded the institute for the Study of Non-Violence in California?

18 Who was back on the chain gang with the Pretenders in 1982?

19 Who had a hit with 'Gloria'?

20 With whom did this singer appear on 'Dead Ringer For Love'?

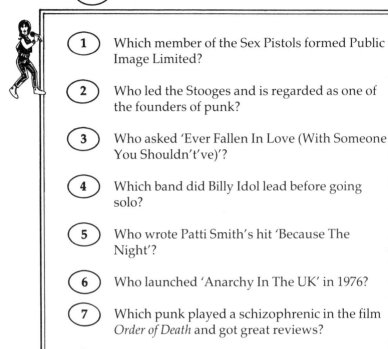

1 Which member of the Sex Pistols formed Public Image Limited?

2 Who led the Stooges and is regarded as one of the founders of punk?

3 Who asked 'Ever Fallen In Love (With Someone You Shouldn't've)'?

4 Which band did Billy Idol lead before going solo?

5 Who wrote Patti Smith's hit 'Because The Night'?

6 Who launched 'Anarchy In The UK' in 1976?

7 Which punk played a schizophrenic in the film *Order of Death* and got great reviews?

8 Jimmy Pursey led which punk band?

9 Who had a 'Germ-Free Adolescence'?

10 Which film about punk was directed by Julien Temple of *Absolute Beginners* fame?

11 Which of the Sex Pistols' songs was banned from the charts?

12 What form of dancing did punk music inspire?

13 Which punky lady wanted to be free in 1981?

14 Which of punks' founders had his own hit with 'Buffalo Gals'?

15 Who had a move from the Banshees to the Sex Pistols?

16 Which surname is shared by Joey, Johnny, Dee Dee, Tommy *and* the band they formed?

17 Who was this punk star accused of murdering?

18 Who had their first UK hit with 'White Riot'?

19 Who had a UK hit with 'Sheena Is A Punk Rocker'?

20 Who was the lead singer of the Velvet Underground, often cited as a major punk influence?

1. Which Beatle occasionally called himself Dr Winston O'Boogie?

2. With which band did Gordon Sumner have his first hits?

3. Rogers Nelson are the second names of which star?

4. What did Christopher Hamill become by rearranging the letters of his surname?

5. Which Jane Fonda film featured the character from whom this band took their name?

6. How is Mrs Sean Penn better known?

7. Who was Lieutenant Lush before he became a boy?

8. How did the Jackson 5 alter their name when Jermaine left?

9. Which famous duo started out as Tom and Jerry?

10. How is George O'Dowd better known?

11. Who is nicknamed 'Soul Brother Number One'?

12. Who started life as Declan McManus?

13. Who was born Marvin Lee Aday but opted for something you can get your teeth into?

14. What was Melanie's surname?

15. Which star of the fifties and sixties was born Dino Crocetti?

16. Who became Yosef Islam and in 1981 auctioned off all his posessions?

17. Who started life as Richard Starkey?

18. How is British star Harry Webb better known?

19. What is Marie Osmond's real first name — Marie, Olive or Doris?

20. What was Donovan's real first name?

(1) Who sang 'Don't Give Up On Us Baby' in 1976

(2) Who had a hit with 'Arthur's Theme (Best Tha You Can Do)'?

(3) Which artist had a lightning hit with 'Somethin In The Air'?

(4) Which duo took 'Maneater' up the charts?

(5) Which group had a 1965 hit with 'I'm Alive'?

(6) With which continent did Toto have a 1981 hit

(7) Which group were 'Standing In The Shadows Of Love' in 1967?

(8) To whom did Jimi Hendrix say, 'Hey'?

(9) Which stone rolled out the solo hit 'Je Suis Un Rock Star'?

(10) Which group had 'A Groovy Kind of Love' in 1966?

(11) Which band flew into the charts with 'For You Love'?

(12) Who was 'Wired For Sound' in 1981?

(13) Which band had a hit with 'Eye Of The Tiger'?

(14) Who had a hit with 'Walk On By' in 1964?

(15) Which trumpet player took 'Hello Dolly' up the charts?

(16) Which singer had a controversial US hit with 'Sugar Walls'?

(17) Who had a UK number one with 'You're The First, The Last, My Everything'?

18 Who is this singer, who had a 1966 hit with 'Distant Drums'?

19 Who did Dexy's Midnight Runners urge to 'come on'?

20 Which singer had success 'Looking Through The Eyes Of Love' in 1965?

1 What honour has Bob Geldof just received in this picture?

2 In which month did the Live Aid concert take place?

3 Which famous actor introduced many of the American bands?

4 From which country did the band Autograph broadcast?

(5) Who sang Elton John's 'Don't Let The Sun Go Down On Me'?

(6) In which city was the American half of the concert staged?

(7) Who played piano for 'Every Breath You Take'?

(8) Who made his appearance in a wheelchair with Ashford and Simpson?

(9) Who sang 'Rebel Rebel' and 'Modern Love'?

(10) What was the longest amount of time allotted to any British act — 13, 15 or 17 minutes?

(11) Who appeared at both the British and American ends of the concert?

(12) What colour shirt does Mick Jagger wear in the 'Dancing In The Street' video?

(13) Who sang 'Love Makes The World Go Round'?

(14) Which duo were joined on stage by Eddie Kendricks and Dave Ruffin?

(15) Who sang 'A View To A Kill'?

(16) Which singer followed Tina Turner and Mick Jagger's act?

(17) Who sang with Black Sabbath?

(18) Which two Rolling Stones backed Bob Dylan?

(19) From which city did Yu Rock Mission broadcast live — Belgrade, Vienna or The Hague?

(20) Which was the first American act to appear after the UK finale?

1 What was the title of Esther and Abi Ofarim's only UK number one hit?

2 Which number one hit singer/songwriter recorded 'Glory Be To God For The Golden Pills', a song in praise of birth control pills?

3 Which Tommy James and the Shondells UK number one was inspired by a sign for the Mutual of New York Insurance Company?

4 Who had a 1980 hit with a song called 'De Do Do Do, De Da Da Da'?

5 Who wrote 'Ob-La-Di, Ob-La-Da' which gave Marmalade a number one in the UK?

6 Who had a 1966 hit with 'Sha La La La Lee'?

7 Which two words completed the title of Rocky Sharpe and the Replay's 1978 hit 'Rama Lama'?

8 Who took 'Da Doo Ron Ron' to the top?

9 Which band had lots of sugar in their 'Co-Co' in 1971?

10 Which naughty comedian had a hit with 'Ernie (The Fastest Milkman In The West)'?

11 What was Jim Stafford's hit girl called?

12 Who urged everyone to 'Turn! Turn! Turn!'?

13 Which frog had a 1977 hit with 'Halfway Down The Stairs'?

14 Bobby 'Boris' Pickett and the Crypt Kickers had which 'monster' hit?

15 Who wrote home with 'Hello Muddah, Hello Faddah'?

16 Which 1968 hit gave Ohio Express love in their tummies?

17 Which rock star recorded 'The Laughing Gnome'?

18 Which teeny-bopper band had a hit with 'Shang-A-Lang'?

19 Which Ray Stevens song was about a man who exposed himself in public places?

20 Which of this star's songs includes the words, 'Tom bo li de say di moi ya, yeah, jambo jumbo'?

1 Who was lead singer of the Animals?

2 Which hard rock band's leader escaped from East Germany at the age of 14?

3 Which band did this singer lead from 1969–75?

4 Who bosses about the E Street Band?

5 Which band was led by John Belushi and Dan Aykroyd?

6 Who was lead guitarist with Cream?

(7) Who died in a Parisian bath in 1971, leaving the 'door' open for a new lead singer?

(8) Who is lead singer of the Who?

(9) Robert Plant was lead singer with which band until 1980?

(10) Which rock star was backed, in one of his incarnations, by the Spiders from Mars?

(11) Who sang 'All Right Now' with Free?

(12) Which British singer/songwriter is backed by the Attractions?

(13) Who was backed by the Jordanaires?

(14) Who was lead singer with the Q-Tips before going solo?

(15) Which band is fronted by Huey Lewis?

(16) Who fronts the Magic Band?

(17) What is Sly's backing group?

(18) Who was lead singer with the Ronettes?

(19) With which band did David Gates make lots of dough?

(20) Which pair of singers fronted Vinegar Joe?

1 Who collapsed, and later died, while reading a book called *The Scientific Search for the Face of Jesus*?

2 Which pop star's funeral tributes included a large white swan?

3 Which killer recorded with Brian and Dennis Wilson of the Beach Boys?

4 Which pop star was honoured by an official wreath of flowers from the Soviet Union?

5 What book was John Lennon's killer reading when he was arrested?

6 Who was shot in a Los Angeles motel in 1964 by a woman who claimed that he had attacked her?

7 Who was killed in a car driven by Gloria Jones on 16 September 1977?

8 Where did Jimi Hendrix appear in concert for the last time?

9 Which member of the Who died of a drug overdose in 1978?

10 In whose London home was the musician Michael Rudetski found dead in August 1986?

11 At a concert by which star did John Lennon make his last stage appearance?

12 What caused Janis Joplin's death?

13 Which member of Led Zeppelin died in 1980, precipitating the end of the band?

14 How did Buddy Holly die?

15 What was the name of the man who shot this star?

16 'God saw that he needed some rest and called him home to be with him' — this is the tombstone inscription of which star?

17 Which Rolling Stone was found dead in a swimming-pool on 3 July 1969?

18 Which member of the Mama and the Papas died in 1974?

19 In which room of his house did Elvis Presley die?

20 Which Beach Boy drowned in 1983?

1 How many Top Ten singles, in the UK and the US, did this star take from his best-selling album?

2 Who joined Captain Daryl Dragon for 'Do That To Me One More Time'?

3 Which song became the best-selling single in British pop history when it overtook the sales of 'Mull Of Kintyre' in 1984?

4 Who, in 1984, became the first British artist to have number ones as a soloist, part of a duo, a trio, a quartet and a quintet?

5 With which duo did Alison Moyet enjoy success before going solo?

6 Who had a hit with 'Everybody Wants To Rule The World'?

7 How many Taylors were there in Duran Duran's original line-up?

8 Who was the lead singer who took Kajagoogoo into the charts with 'Too Shy'?

9 What, according to Annie Lennox of Eurythmics, were the first words that her partner Dave Stewart said to her?

10 How many Thompson Twins are there?

11 Who had a hit album with *No Parlez*?

12 What do girls want, according to Cyndi Lauper?

13 With which soliloquy from *Hamlet* did Mel Brooks have a 1984 hit?

14 Which lady, famous for her 'thunderous thighs', had a 1984 hit with 'I Feel For You'?

15 Which Duran Duran hit was a number one in both the UK and the US?

16 Who had a 1985 hit with 'Run To You'?

17 Whose 'Rebel Yell' took him into the 1985 charts?

18 What appears in brackets after the Culture Club hit 'Time'?

19 Who sang about 'The Boy In The Bubble'?

20 Which Duran Duran video was banned because of its naked girls?

1 What was M's 1979 hit?

2 Which crooner joined the Andrews Sisters for 'Pistol Packin' Mama'?

3 Which singer made her screen debut in *Mad Max III*?

4 Which group made the Top Twenty for the first time in 1966 with 'Hold Tight'?

5 Who was '(Sitting On) The Dock Of The Bay' for a 1968 hit?

6 Which sexy US songstress had a UK number one with 'The Power Of Love'?

7 Who had a hit with 'I'm A Boy'?

8 Which youngster had a 1984 hit with 'Too Late For Goodbyes'?

9 Which 1962 instrumental hit was the first record by a British group to top the US pop charts?

10 Who transferred 'Chanson D'Amour' into a UK number one in 1977?

11 What did the Shangri-Las walk in and Pat Boone write in?

12 Who provided the macabre voice-overs at the end of the single 'Thriller'?

13 Who had a 1965 hit with 'Make It Easy On Yourself'?

14 What were Ike and Tina Turner's 'limits'?

15 What kind of roses took Marie Osmond into the charts in 1973?

16 What did the initials of Michael Jackson's 'P. Y. T.' stand for?

17 At which hotel did the Eagles stay in 1977?

18 Who shared Elton John's hit 'Don't Go Breaking My Heart'?

19 What appeared in brackets after the Four Seasons hit 'December 1963'?

20 What was this popular singer's first hit?

(1) Which of this group's hits was adapted from a Coca-Cola commercial?

(2) Which 1967 song was based on the Bach cantata *Sleepers Awake*?

(3) Which American cop TV series gave Mike Post a 1981 hit?

(4) Which classical composer featured in the title of Falco's 1985 hit?

(5) From which rock musical did Yvonne Elliman take her hit 'I Don't Know How To Love Him'?

(6) What was the 1968 classical instrumental from Mason Williams?

(7) Who used a wobbleboard on his hit 'Tie Me Kangaroo Down, Sport'?

(8) Which orchestra had a hit with 'Hooked On Classics'?

9 Which Emerson, Lake and Palmer album was based on a classical work by the composer Mussorgsky?

10 Which passionate French record was banned because of its heavy breathing?

11 Which group had a hit with 'I Hear A Symphony' in 1965?

12 Which TV show about an all-girl rock group starred Julie Covington, Charlotte Cornwell and Rula Lenska?

13 Which famous Scottish anthem was taken into the charts by the Pipes and Drums and Military Band of the Royal Scots Dragoon Guards?

14 On which theme from Gustav Holst's *Planets Suite* did Manfred Mann's Earth Band base their 'Joybringer'?

15 Which composer had hits with themes from *E. T.*, *Star Wars* and *Close Encounters of the Third Kind*?

16 Who is the classical guitarist who took 'Cavatina' up the charts?

17 Who had a UK hit with 'Birdie Song (Birdie Dance)'?

18 On which book of the Bible was the Byrds 'Turn! Turn! Turn!' based?

19 Elaine Paige and Barbara Dickson's hit 'I Know Him So Well' came from which musical?

20 Which Scottish comedian had a hit with a parody of Tammy Wynette's 'D.I.V.O.R.C.E.'?

1 What laid-back colour gave this singer a hit in 1967?

2 What colour was Joni Mitchell's cab?

3 Who were 'Black Skin Blue Eyed Boys' in 1970?

4 What colour Christmas did Elvis Presley have in 1974?

5 What kind of sugar took the Rolling Stones up the charts?

6 What colour was Prince's little Corvette?

7 Who had a hit with 'The Green Manalishi (With The Two-Pronged Crown)'?

8 What colour was the Lemon Piper's tambourine?

9 What colour was the Rolling Stones small rooster?

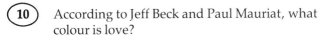

10 According to Jeff Beck and Paul Mauriat, what colour is love?

11 Which 'Mr' gave the Electric Light Orchestra a 1978 hit?

12 What colour did the Rolling Stones paint it in 1966?

13 What colour wine gave Jimmy James and the Vagabonds and U.B.40 their hits?

14 What colour were Nena's 99 balloons?

15 What colour was the machine that took Hawkwind to the top?

16 What colour was the Beatles' submarine?

17 What colourful lady made a medicinal compound, according to a Scaffold hit?

18 What colour haze surrounded the Jimi Hendrix Experience?

19 What wedding gave Billy Idol a 1983 US hit?

20 What colour was the angel that Roy Orbison and Gene Pitney sang about?

1 What colour was the Cadillac Elvis bought his mother in 1956?

2 Who is the man shown with Elvis Presley in the picture?

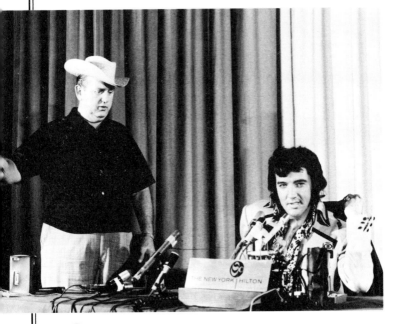

3 Which song did Elvis, Dorothy Squires, Frank Sinatra and the Sex Pistols all record?

4 What was Elvis's first film?

5 What was Graceland before it was turned into Elvis's mansion home?

6 Which of Elvis's songs contains spoken lines from Shakespeare?

7 What was Elvis's first UK hit?

(8) What was Elvis's middle name?

(9) Which Beatle said, 'I basically became a musician because of Elvis Presley'?

(10) How many children did Elvis father?

(11) Which of his films was delayed when Elvis inhaled one of his dental crowns?

(12) What army rank did Elvis hold by the time he was discharged?

(13) Which Elvis record was Paul McCartney's number one *Desert Island Discs* choice?

(14) On what street does Heartbreak Hotel stand?

(15) Which film introduced the song 'Can't Help Falling In Love'?

(16) Which of Elvis's hits was an adaption of a German folk song entitled 'Muss I Denn'?

(17) Which Elvis film was based on a book written by Harold Robbins?

(18) Which of Elvis's hits had the B side 'I Gotta Know'?

(19) What part does Elvis's widow play in *Dallas*?

(20) Who had a hit with 'I Remember Elvis Presley'?

1 Which blind guitarist and singer was caught trying to smuggle a Braille edition of *Playboy* into South Africa?

2 What did David Bowie announce to the press on 22 January 1972?

3 Whose hair caught fire while he was filming a Pepsi advert?

4 Which Monkee was threatened with drafting to Vietnam?

5 Which member of the Mamas and the Papas was arrested in Southampton for stealing from a London hotel?

6 Who left George Harrison to marry Eric Clapton?

7 What religion is Michael Jackson?

8 Who said, on becoming engaged to Miss Vicki, 'I shed a tear and put it in an envelope that I always keep in my ukelele'?

9 Who caused a scandal by saying, 'Jesus was all right but his disciples were thick and ordinary'?

10 Which member of the Rolling Stones once boasted he'd bedded 64 groupies in one month?

11 Who married Alana Hamilton in 1979?

12 Which male pop star was rated number ten on a 1973 list of worst-dressed women?

13 Which Beach Boy joined murderer Charles Manson in his orgies?

14 Who ditched Bryan Ferry for Mick Jagger?

15 Who was Dr Meg Patterson's most famous patient in 1986?

16 How much was Brian Epstein's cut of the Beatles' revenue?

17 Which Canadian politician's wife became involved with the Rolling Stones?

18 Which punk said, 'Love is two minutes fifty seconds of squishing noises'?

19 Who was engaged to Paul McCartney but didn't marry him?

20 In which city did these two stage their first 'Bed In'?

(1)   Which of these brothers had a hit with 'Another Lonely Night In New York'?

(2)   Which singer was Real Madrid's reserve goalkeeper?

(3)   Which of Elizabeth Taylor's husbands had a hit with 'Oh Mein Papa'?

(4)   Which member of the Boone family had a 1979 hit with 'You Light Up My Life'?

(5)   Who raced solo up the charts with 'Cars'?

(6)   From which group did Agnetha Faltskog break loose?

(7)   Who had a hit with 'The Belle Of St Mark'?

8. Which British songstress hit the big time after appearing on a TV show called *The Big Time*?

9. Who was 'Busted' in 1963?

10. Who had a 1984 hit with 'Caribbean Queen (No More Love On The Run)'?

11. Which Supremes hit gave Phil Collins a solo number one hit in 1983?

12. Who had a 1974 hit with 'And I Love You So'?

13. What was Madonna's first Top Twenty hit?

14. Which Bing Crosby record originally entered the US pop charts in 1942 and re-entered for 18 more seasons?

15. Who wrote and had a hit with 'Love Theme From A Star Is Born (Evergreen)'?

16. Who went down 'Electric Avenue' and into the charts on his own?

17. Who wanted to wake up with you in 1986?

18. Whose 'New Song' gave him his first chart hit?

19. What was the 'name' of Toni Basil's chart topper?

20. Who sang about 'Delta Dawn' in 1973?

1 Which group had a hit with 'Save The Last Dance For Me' in 1960?

2 Who climbed the charts in the company of 'Gypsies, Tramps And Thieves'?

3 Which duo were on 'Top Of The World' in 1973?

4 Which group hit the charts with 'Let's Spend The Night Together'?

5 Who had a hit with 'Give Me Just A Little More Time' in 1970?

6 Who had 'Subterranean Homesick Blues' in 1965?

7 From which of his albums did Bruce Springsteen take the single 'Cover Me'?

8 Which oriental-sounding band sang about 'Dance Hall Days' in 1984?

9 Who picked a fine time to leave Kenny Rogers according to one of his songs?

10 Who sang 'Like A Virgin' without looking like one?

11 What, according to a Connie Francis hit, told a tale on you?

12 Which boys had a 1984 hit with 'Wild Boys'?

13 Who climbed the charts with 'Dance Away'?

14 Which Wham! song reached number one in both the UK and the US?

15 What did Tina Turner say we didn't need another of in her 1985 hit?

16 Which group had chart success with 'Sweet Dreams Are Made Of This'?

17 What two-letter word is found in the title of four of the Beatles' first eight singles?

18 Which actor sang 'As Time Goes By' in the classic film *Casablanca* and had a UK hit with it in 1977?

19 Which twins had a hit with 'Sisters Of Mercy'?

20 What was the title of this man's only US Top Twenty hit?

1 Who took the theme from *Star Wars* into the charts?

2 Who had success with *Tubular Bells*?

3 Which great band leader died in 1944 when his plane disappeared on a flight from France to England?

4 Where did Horst Janowski take a walk?

5 Which Greek gave Herb Alpert and the Tijuana Brass and Marcello Minerbi their hits?

6 Which of this rocker's hits was instrumental only?

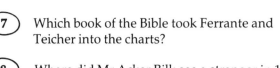

7 Which book of the Bible took Ferrante and Teicher into the charts?

8 Where did Mr Acker Bilk see a stranger in 1962?

9 Which theme from the film *2001: A Space Odyssey* did Deodato take into the charts in 1973?

10 Which rhyming band had magical success with 'Hocus Pokus'?

11 What colour were Booker T. and the MG's instrumental onions?

12 What was Fleetwood Mac's UK instrumental hit?

13 Which quartet 'took five' in 1961?

14 Who wrote 'The Entertainer', which gave Marvin Hamlisch a 1974 hit?

15 Who played 'Annie's Song' on his golden flute?

16 Which Clint Eastwood movie gave Hugo Montenegro a hit in 1968?

17 Who conducted 'Love's Theme' for the Love Unlimited Orchestra?

18 Which band had a hit with 'FBI'?

19 Which average kind of band took 'Pick Up The Pieces' into the charts?

20 Which trio created 'Fanfare For The Common Man'?

1 What physical attribute did this songstress want in her 1982 hit?

2 Who were *Brothers in Arms*?

3 What part of the anatomy did ZZ Top take into the US charts in 1984?

4) Who had a 1979 hit with 'Angel Eyes'?

5) What was Imagination's first hit?

6) Who got 'Physical' in 1981?

7) Who was 'Breathless' in 1958?

8) What kind of heart did Blondie have?

9) Who had a hit with 'Fat Bottomed Girls'?

10) What did Jackson Browne and the Jackson Five consult the doctor about in 1972 and 1973?

11) Who had a hit with 'Hotlegs'?

12) Where did Brenda Lee have her heart in 1962?

13) Who had a hit with 'Eyes Without A Face'?

14) What, according to one of Fats Waller's hits, were too big?

15) What were Police wrapped around in 1983?

16) Who had a hit with 'Footloose'?

17) What was the fourteen-word title of the Bellamy Brothers' last hit?

18) Who took 'Goldfinger' up the charts?

19) What part of the anatomy did the Beatles want to hold?

20) Who had a 1982 'Heart Attack'?

1 Who appeared on stage as Jumping Jack Flash?

2 Which British psychedelic rock band was the first to use a sound and light show?

3 Who initially performed only in a mackintosh but eventually settled for a purple raincoat and black underpants?

4 Who set light to his guitar at the Monterey pop festival?

5 Who recorded 'Caroline (Live At The N.E.C.)'?

6 Who was famous for chopping up baby dolls and hanging himself on stage?

7 Which band made a habit of destroying their equipment at the end of their concerts in the sixties?

8 Who was banned after splitting his trousers once too often?

9 Which lead singer was charged with indecent exposure after a performance in Miami in 1969?

10 Which rock pianist is famed for his custom-made glasses?

11 Who gave a free concert in Central Park to raise money for a children's playground, and ended up making a loss?

12 Who appeared on the Ed Sullivan TV show — but only from the waist up?

13 Which country music star found himself on stage as a temporary Beach Boy when Brian Wilson had a breakdown?

(14) Who did the Youth Federation of China invite to perform in Peking in 1985?

(15) Who received a fee of $1·5 million for one show in San Bernadino County, California, on 26 May 1983?

(16) Did Jimi Hendrix perform at Woodstock?

(17) Who was performing when Meredith Hunter was killed at the Altamont Festival?

(18) Who performed each week on the Andy Williams TV show?

(19) Who wore a frock and quoted Shelley at a free concert in Hyde Park on 3 July 1969?

(20) Which of his characters is David Bowie playing here?

(1) What was the name of this rocker's band?

(2) What originally appeared in brackets after 'Rock Around The Clock'?

(3) Who never felt more like singing the blues in 1956?

(4) What was the Everly Brothers' first hit?

(5) Which American rock and roll star died when his taxi hit a lamppost in Chippenham, Wiltshire, England in 1958?

(6) Who set the world alight with 'Great Balls Of Fire'?

7. Which guitarist had the motto 'Have twangy guitar, will travel'?

8. Which furious British rocker got only halfway to paradise?

9. Who made Beethoven roll over?

10. Which mascara-wearing, piano-pounding rocker abandoned rock and roll in 1957 after seeing a vision and promising God he would change his ways?

11. Which rocker's fans copied his limp, caused by a Navy motorcycle accident?

12. Who took Sally and Miss Molly to the top of the charts?

13. Who was the third rocker to die in the accident that killed Buddy Holly and the Big Bopper?

14. Which man of iron is widely thought to be the first British rock and roll star?

15. Who had a hit with 'Blue Suede Shoes' before Elvis Presley?

16. Who made his 'duckwalk' famous?

17. Which enduring British singer had his first rock and roll hit with 'Move It'?

18. What dance took the world by storm after Prince Serge Obolensky was seen dancing it in the Peppermint Lounge, Manhattan?

19. Who was the King of Skiffle?

20. Who was the first to write love letters in the sand?

1 Who was the Kinks' lead singer?

2 Who replaced Peter Gabriel as lead singer of Genesis?

3 Who is the Communards' lead singer?

4 Who led the Tremeloes until 1966?

5 With which band of the seventies did Leslie McKeown roll to success?

6 Who is lead singer of Frankie Goes To Hollywood?

7 With which band did Annabella Lwin wow the world?

8 Who was lead singer with Mott the Hoople?

9 With which band did Tony Hadley find fame?

10 Who was lead singer with Manfred Mann in the sixties?

11 Which singer appeared with Jennifer Warnes on 'Up Where We Belong'?

12 Who was the vocalist in Them?

13 Which singer was nearly killed when his yacht, *Drum*, overturned in 1985?

14 Who is lead singer with the Pretenders?

15 Who left the Equals to pursue a successful solo career?

16 Which singer once said in an interview that she owned 96 pairs of glasses?

(17) Which duo had a hit in 1982 singing, 'I Can't Go For That (No Can Do)'?

(18) Who is this band's male lead singer?

(19) Who had hits with 'I Never Loved A Man (The Way I Love You)' and 'I Say A Little Prayer'?

(20) Who had a hit with 'Jolene'?

(1) Which European capital gave this band a hit in 1981?

(2) Who sang 'I've Gotta Get A Message To You' in 1968?

(3) Who complained about 'My Perfect Cousin' in 1980?

(4) Who had a hit with 'Return To Sender'?

(5) Who sang about 'Puff The Magic Dragon'?

(6) Which band had their last hit with 'Metal Guru'?

(7) Who took 'Rag Doll' up the charts in 1964?

(8) What is the name of Frank Zappa's daughter, who entered the US charts with 'Valley Girls' in 1982?

(9) Who had a 1964 hit with 'Tobacco Road'?

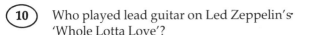

10 Who played lead guitar on Led Zeppelin's 'Whole Lotta Love'?

11 Who sang along with Cliff Richard on his remake of 'Living Doll' in 1986?

12 Which Beatle made it on his own up the charts with 'Back Off Boogaloo'?

13 Who took 'Tell Her About It' up the charts?

14 Which Middle East leader is mentioned in 'Where Do You Go To My Lovely'?

15 Who had a 1985 hit with 'Nikita'?

16 With which song did Nancy Sinatra stroll through the charts in 1966?

17 Who scaled the charts with 'River Deep, Mountain High'?

18 Who had a 1964 hit with 'I'm Into Something Good'?

19 Who had a number one with 'When I Need You' in 1977?

20 What was this star's second UK hit?

1 What is the only colour Johnny Cash wears on stage?

2 Which Tennessee town is accepted as the Country Capital of the US?

3 Who had a 1977 hit with 'Don't It Make My Brown Eyes Blue'?

4 Which country rock star married Kris Kristofferson in 1973?

5 Which singer and songwriter suffered from Huntingdon's Chorea and was visited in hospital by Bob Dylan?

6 What is tattooed on Glen Campbell's arm?

7 What number follows country star George Hamilton's name?

8 Who was known as Little Miss Dynamite when her first record entered the charts at the age of 15?

9 Which TV show's theme gave Waylon Jennings a 1980 US hit?

10 Which country singer admits to a bust measurement 'in the low forties'?

11 Which Monkee has had country hits with the First and Second National Bands?

12 Which country singer was married at 13 and became a grandmother at 32?

13 Who had hits with songs about Galveston, Wichita and Phoenix, among others?

14 Who cashed in with the hit 'I Walk The Line'?

15 Who had a 1974 hit with 'Behind Closed Doors'?

16 Who is Crystal Gayle's famous country-singing sister?

17 Which group had a hit with John Denver's song 'Leavin' On A Jet Plane'?

18 Which country star was the subject of the film *Coal Miner's Daughter*?

19 Which country-pop singer starred with Sylvester Stallone in *Rhinestone*?

20 What did this star 'Thank God' for making him?

THE ANSWERS

1 · WM · NAMES

1. Mrs Robinson — the picture shows Simon and Garfunkel
2. Bridget the Midget
3. Maggie
4. Jude
5. Billie Joe
6. Barbara Ann
7. The Everly Brothers
8. Jane
9. Annie
10. Marie
11. Joe DiMaggio
12. Diane
13. Peggy Sue
14. Ben
15. Bananarama
16. Sylvia's
17. Rosie and Caroline respectively
18. 'Roxanne'
19. Oliver's
20. Mrs Brown — the picture shows Herman's Hermits

2 · S · THE BEATLES

1. *Abbey Road*
2. 'Yesterday'
3. Ringo
4. Vera, Chuck and Dave
5. 'I Want To Hold Your Hand'
6. The Cavern Club
7. Paul McCartney
8. A Granny Smith
9. No
10. *Help!*
11. Brian Epstein
12. Paul McCartney and Ringo Starr
13. John Lennon
14. Ringo Starr
15. Bob Dylan
16. James
17. Ringo Starr
18. 'Please Please Me'
19. *Rubber Soul*
20. George Harrison

3 · R · IT'S ONLY ROCK'N'ROLL

1. Joan Jett
2. Billy Joel
3. The Sex Pistols
4. Jimmy Carter — the picture shows Bob Dylan
5. Bruce Springsteen
6. The Ramones
7. Status Quo
8. David Essex
9. The Clash
10. King — 'Rock'N'Roll Is King'
11. David Bowie
12. Gary Glitter
13. Michael Jackson
14. Elvis Presley
15. Freddie Mercury
16. The Righteous Brothers
17. B. Bumble and the Stingers
18. The Moody Blues
19. Bill Haley and the Comets
20. 'Crocodile Rock'

4 · P · THE SWINGING SIXTIES

1. The Seekers
2. 'Telstar'
3. Tiny Tim
4. Ray Charles
5. 'Sunny Afternoon'
6. *Revolver*
7. Neil Diamond
8. Frank and Nancy Sinatra
9. The Beatles
10. Wayne Fontana
11. The Beatles
12. An 'Itsy Bitsy Teeny Weeny Yellow Polkadot Bikini'
13. Little Eva
14. 'Dominique'
15. 'Do Wah Diddy Diddy'
16. Petula Clark
17. Freddie and the Dreamers
18. Sonny and Cher
19. The Archies
20. 'Puppet On A String' — the picture shows Sandie Shaw

5 · RPM · HITS 1

1. 'Bridge Over Troubled Water'
2. Sam Cooke
3. James Brown
4. Madonna
5. *Brothers In Arms* — the picture shows Dire Straits
6. Deep Purple
7. The Young Rascals
8. 'Bohemian Rhapsody'
9. Diana Ross
10. The Mamas and the Papas
11. Elvis Presley
12. September
13. Laurel and Hardy
14. Michael Jackson
15. Art Garfunkel
16. The Psychedelic Furs
17. Lou Reed
18. Stephen Stills
19. The Crystals
20. Bread

6 · MW · THE MOVIES

1. Ray Parker Jr — the picture shows the film *Ghostbusters*
2. *Saturday Night Fever*
3. *Yellow Submarine*
4. *South Pacific*
5. *Rocky III*
6. *Paint Your Wagon*
7. Kris Kristofferson
8. *A Hard Day's Night*
9. Irene Cara
10. 'Up Where We Belong'
11. Dolly Parton
12. Billie Holiday
13. Cher
14. Mr Lawrence — *Merry Christmas Mr Lawrence*
15. Bob Dylan
16. Mick Jagger
17. *Don't Knock the Rock*
18. *ABBA — The Movie*
19. *Midnight Cowboy*
20. *Expresso Bongo* — the picture shows Cliff Richard

7 · WM · WORLD TITLES

1. New York
2. Argentina
3. The Mull of Kintyre
4. Chicago — the picture shows Frank Sinatra
5. New Orleans
6. Massachusetts
7. Liverpool
8. Scarborough Fair
9. Ipanema
10. Clarkesville
11. America
12. 'California Girls'
13. France
14. China
15. West Virginia
16. Georgia
17. Spain
18. Amarillo
19. London
20. A New Jersey — from the song 'Delaware'

8 · S · PIONEERS

1. Paul McCartney
2. The first proper rock and roll record
3. Chuck Berry
4. Gene Vincent
5. 'Summertime Blues'
6. It was the day Buddy Holly died
7. Bo Diddley
8. Fats Domino
9. Don and Phil
10. Chuck Berry
11. Jerry Lee Lewis
12. Dave Dee
13. Miss Molly
14. The Hollies
15. Roy Orbison
16. Alvin Stardust
17. Bill Haley
18. 'It Doesn't Matter Anymore'
19. Jerry Lee Lewis
20. Sam Cooke

9 · R · GLAMOUR AND GLITTER

1. Roxy Music
2. Smile
3. David Bowie
4. Gary Glitter
5. T. Rex
6. Labelle
7. David Bowie
8. Kiss
9. Sweet
10. Boney M
11. Michael Jackson
12. Gary Glitter
13. Freddie Mercury
14. Kiss
15. Genesis
16. Village People
17. David Bowie
18. Queen
19. Adam and the Ants
20. Reginald Dwight — the picture shows Elton John

11 · RPM · HITS 2

1. 'What's Love Got To Do With It?' — the picture shows Tina Turner
2. 'Hey Jude'
3. Harry Chapin
4. Fourth
5. The Carpenters
6. Cat Stevens
7. Yazoo
8. Bill Haley
9. 'Trains And Boats And Planes'
10. Monday
11. Gary Puckett
12. Kim Wilde
13. Stevie Wonder
14. Ringo
15. Donovan
16. 'American Pie'
17. 'The Marrakesh Express'
18. 'Wild Thing'
19. The Everly Brothers
20. 'Angie'

10 · P · THE SEVENTIES

1. 'Two Little Boys'
2. The Smurfs
3. A rose garden
4. Bachman-Turner Overdrive
5. Bad Company
6. Paul Simon
7. Phil Lynott
8. 10CC
9. Stepmother-stepson
10. The words
11. 'You've Got A Friend'
12. Melanie
13. *Play Misty For Me*
14. Leo Sayer
15. Helen Reddy
16. 'Amazing Grace'
17. The Hollies
18. Canned Heat
19. 'Another Brick In The Wall'
20. 461 — the picture shows Eric Clapton with Lionel Richie

12 · MW · FOLK

1. James Taylor and Carly Simon
2. Simon and Garfunkel
3. Peter and Gordon
4. 'Big Yellow Taxi'
5. Peter, Paul and Mary
6. Dylan Thomas
7. The Mamas and the Papas
8. 'Streets Of London'
9. Donovan
10. Melanie
11. Bob Dylan
12. Mick Jagger
13. Pete Seeger
14. Judy Collins
15. George Harrison
16. Bob Dylan
17. The Seekers
18. Peter, Paul and Mary
19. The clowns
20. Bob Dylan — the picture is of Joan Baez

13 · WM · DEDICATED TO…

1. Marilyn Monroe
2. John Lennon
3. Julian Lennon
4. Warren Beatty
5. 'American Pie' — the picture shows Buddy Holly with the Crickets
6. Geno Washington
7. Bette Davis
8. Abraham Lincoln, Martin Luther King and John F. Kennedy
9. Martin Luther King
10. Don McLean
11. Buddy Holly
12. Carole King
13. Frank Lloyd Wright
14. Marvin Gaye and Jackie Wilson
15. Eva Peron
16. Alexander Graham Bell
17. Ann Deutschendorf, ex-wife of John Deutschendorf/Denver
18. Harry Truman
19. Princess Margaret and Lord Snowdon
20. Paul McCartney — in 'How Do You Sleep?'

14 · S · BANDS

1. Pete Best — the picture shows the Beatles
2. The Blockheads
3. Steve Harley
4. The Miracles
5. Joan Jett
6. Bob Seger
7. The Dakotas
8. Kid Creole
9. Booker T.
10. Aphrodite's Child
11. Bob Dylan
12. John Mayall's
13. Ultravox
14. The Animals
15. The Teenagers
16. Martha Reeves
17. T. Rex
18. Frank Zappa
19. The Monkees
20. The Pacemakers

15 · R · HEAVY STUFF

1. A billion dollars
2. Iron Maiden
3. Deep Purple
4. William Burroughs
5. Status Quo
6. Jimmy Page
7. Deep Purple
8. Greg Lake
9. ZZ Top
10. Ozzy Osbourne
11. Led Zeppelin
12. ZZ Top
13. King Crimson
14. Judas Priest
15. Deep Purple
16. Jimmy Page
17. Ozzy Osbourne
18. Australia
19. Steppenwolf
20. David Lee Roth

16 · P · WORDS

1. 'Jailhouse Rock'
2. 'Daydream Believer'
3. 'All You Need Is Love'
4. 'You've Got A Friend'
5. Rod Stewart
6. 'I'll Never Find Another You'
7. 'From Me To You'
8. 'Strangers In The Night'
9. 'Homeward Bound'
10. 'Here Comes The Sun'
11. '1.2.3.'
12. 'Those Were The Days'
13. 'Ticket To Ride'
14. 'Will You Still Love Me Tomorrow?'
15. 'I Got You Babe'
16. 'Can't Help Falling In Love With You'
17. 'I Get Around'
18. 'My Way'
19. 'Matthew And Son'
20. Yellow

17 · RPM · HITS 3

1. The Bee Gees
2. Percy Sledge
3. Johnny Cash
4. 'Reet Petite'
5. Al Stewart
6. Michael Jackson and Paul McCartney
7. The Supremes
8. Phil Everly and Cliff Richard
9. Manfred Mann
10. Chris de Burgh
11. The Crystals
12. 'Hit The Road Jack'
13. Dionne Warwick
14. Buddy Holly
15. Elton John
16. 'Strawberry Fields'
17. The Temptations
18. The Ronettes
19. 'Rock Around The Clock'
20. 'Relax' — the picture shows Frankie Goes To Hollywood

18 · MW · MOTOWN

1. Mary Wells
2. Berry Gordy Jr
3. Smokey Robinson and the Miracles
4. Little Stevie Wonder
5. Syreeta
6. Marvin Gaye
7. Detroit
8. The Supremes
9. Phil Collins
10. Lionel Richie
11. The Temptations
12. The Jackson 5
13. 1984
14. *The Woman in Red*
15. Smokey Robinson and the Miracles
16. The Four Tops
17. Stevie Wonder
18. 'Tammy'
19. 'I Can't Help Myself'
20. Stevie Wonder

19 · WM · MUSIC BY NUMBERS

1. 2525 — from 'In The Year 2525'
2. 24
3. 9 to 5
4. 50
5. 48
6. Sixteen
7. Three
8. Two
9. 10538
10. *Six Pack*
11. Three
12. Nineteenth
13. One
14. Eight
15. 5.15
16. 59th Street Bridge
17. Seven
18. 99
19. Nineteen
20. 1984 — the picture shows Eurythmics, who wrote the song for the film of *1984*, which was written by George Orwell

20 · S · GUITAR HEROES

1. Twang — the picture shows Duane Eddy, known as the King of Twang
2. Denny Laine
3. Ritchie Blackmore
4. Bo Diddley
5. Graham Nash
6. Pete Townsend
7. The Shadows
8. The Clash
9. Eric Clapton
10. Duane
11. Dave Gilmour
12. Eric Clapton
13. Pete Townsend
14. Jimi Hendrix
15. Astronomy
16. Eddie Van Halen
17. Paul Kossof
18. Jimi Hendrix
19. Ronnie Lane
20. Jimmy Page

21 · R · NEW WAVE

1. Stewart Copeland
2. Talking Heads
3. Eurythmics
4. U2
5. 'Call Me'
6. Bruce Springsteen
7. Police
8. Major Tom
9. David and Mark Knopfler
10. Soft Cell
11. Billy Joel
12. C. G. Jung
13. Annie Lennox
14. 'Every Breath You Take'
15. Bruce Springsteen
16. Paul Weller
17. *Brothers In Arms*
18. Bob Geldof
19. Sting
20. *Purple Rain*

22 · P · ALBUMS

1. *Graceland*
2. *Sgt Pepper's Lonely Hearts Club Band*
3. Lionel Richie
4. A tiger
5. *Band On The Run* — the picture shows Wings
6. They appeared naked on its sleeve
7. Simon and Garfunkel
8. Frankie Goes to Hollywood
9. Elton John
10. Beatles
11. *Dark Side of the Moon*
12. Phil Collins
13. *John Wesley Harding*
14. Rod Stewart
15. James Taylor
16. *Tommy*
17. The Hindenburg
18. Stevie Wonder
19. Wham!
20. The Rolling Stones

23 · RPM · HITS 4

1. Marvin Gaye
2. Neil Sedaka
3. America
4. *Wuthering Heights*
5. Sue
6. 'Light My Fire'
7. 'Michelle'
8. Anita Ward
9. Britt Ekland
10. Neil Diamond
11. The Ronettes
12. Gloria Gaynor
13. The Beach Boys
14. 'It's Now Or Never'
15. Madonna
16. Your playhouse — 'I'm Gonna Tear Your Playhouse Down'. The picture shows Paul Young
17. 'Mr Tambourine Man'
18. Deniece Williams
19. The Weather Girls
20. 'It's A Miracle'

24 · MW · DISCO

1. 'Love To Love You Baby' — the picture shows Donna Summer
2. 'Born To Be Alive'
3. Chic
4. *Saturday Night Fever*
5. 'Disco Lady'
6. Barbra Streisand
7. *Flashdance*
8. Sister Sledge
9. Gloria Gaynor
10. David Bowie
11. 'MacArthur Park'
12. Italian
13. Gloria Gaynor
14. Wood — 'Knock On Wood'
15. Blondie
16. Donna Summer
17. Trammps
18. KC and the Sunshine Band
19. Bruce Springsteen
20. Chic

25 · WM · I WRITE THE SONGS

1. Lionel Richie
2. John Lennon and Paul McCartney
3. Brian Wilson
4. David Bowie
5. Bernie Taupin
6. 'Happy Birthday'
7. George Michael
8. Pete Seeger
9. 'Tainted Love'
10. Mark Knopfler
11. Howard Jones
12. 'White Christmas'
13. Barry Gibb
14. Charlie Chaplin
15. Michael Jackson and Lionel Richie
16. Ray Davies
17. Bob Geldof
18. Cole Porter
19. Jerry Lieber and Mike Stoller
20. John Lennon and Paul McCartney
    — the picture shows Siouxie and
    the Banshees, who had a hit with
    'Dear Prudence'

26 · S · THE ROLLING STONES

1. Charlie Watts, the drummer
2. 'It's All Over Now'
3. Bill Wyman
4. Lennon and McCartney
5. *Beggar's Banquet*
6. 'Midnight Rambler'
7. Nicaraguan
8. Andy Warhol
9. Mick Taylor
10. An emerald
11. Keith Richards
12. Brian Jones
13. Nicholas Roeg
14. Bill Wyman
15. Altamont
16. Marianne Faithfull
17. Butterflies
18. Tina Turner
19. A zip
20. Mick Jagger

27 · R · MUSIC MAKERS

1. Guitar
2. John Coghlan
3. Keyboards
4. Roxy Music
5. Phil Lynott
6. Drums
7. Fleetwood Mac
8. Kenny Jones
9. Saxophone
10. Ravi Shankar
11. Brian Jones
12. Vangelis
13. Jon Moss
14. The Who
15. Stevie Wonder
16. Karen Carpenter
17. The Stranglers
18. Drums
19. Rick Wakeman
20. B — Andy Summers of Police

28 · P · NUMBER ONE

1. 'Say Say Say' — the picture shows
   Paul McCartney and Michael
   Jackson
2. Vincent Van Gogh
3. 'Message In A Bottle'
4. Helen Shapiro
5. 'The Purple People Eater'
6. The J. Geils Band
7. Serge Gainsbourg
8. 'Do Ya Think I'm Sexy'
9. Jim Croce
10. Gladys Knight and the Pips
11. 'Tie A Yellow Ribbon Round The
    Old Oak Tree'
12. 'Albatross'
13. 'Do They Know It's Christmas?'
14. Chuck Berry
15. Peter Sarstedt
16. '(I Can't Get No) Satisfaction'
17. 'Imagine'
18. 'Endless Love'
19. Vangelis
20. The Bee Gees

29 · RPM · HITS 5

1. Telly Savalas
2. The Crickets
3. 'Walk Away Renee'
4. *Woodstock*
5. Olivia Newton-John
6. *Grease*
7. Kool
8. Frankie Goes To Hollywood
9. Barbra Streisand
10. Tom Jones
11. David Cassidy
12. Foreigner
13. 'My Girl'
14. Saturday Night
15. Philip Bailey — the picture shows Phil Collins
16. The Isley Brothers
17. Queen
18. 'Wherever I Lay My Hat'
19. Police
20. Julio Iglesias

30 · MW · REGGAE

1. Toots
2. Madness
3. 'Johnny Reggae'
4. Rastafarianism
5. The Wailers — the picture shows Bob Marley
6. Desmond Dekker
7. 'Buffalo Soldier'
8. Jimmy Cliff
9. Black Uhuru
10. Paul Simon
11. Desmond Dekker
12. Jamaica
13. Blondie
14. Toots and the Maytals
15. Eric Clapton
16. Althia and Donna
17. Prince Buster
18. Bob Marley
19. Johnny Nash
20. U.B.40

31 · WM · QUOTE...UNQUOTE

1. Chewing Gum
2. 'I Love You'
3. 'Fire And Rain'
4. 'Que Sera Sera'
5. 'Itchycoo'
6. Swing
7. 'Let It Be'
8. 'Leader Of The Pack'
9. 'Substitute'
10. 'Michelle'
11. My blue suede shoes
12. 'Rocket Man'
13. 'Summer Holiday'
14. 'Moon Shadow' — the picture shows Cat Stevens
15. 'Candle In The Wind'
16. Randy Newman
17. Vegemite
18. The Father, Son and Holy Ghost
19. 'The Ballad Of John And Yoko'
20. 'Leaving On A Jetplane'

32 · S · WILD WOMEN

1. Pearl — the picture shows Janis Joplin
2. Linda Ronstadt
3. Stevie Nicks
4. Annie Lennox
5. Diana Ross
6. Maureen Tucker
7. Janis Joplin
8. Deborah Harry
9. Toyah
10. Velvet Underground
11. A hero — 'Holding Out For A Hero'
12. Grace Slick
13. Janis Joplin
14. Linda Ronstadt
15. Tina Turner
16. Suzi Quatro
17. Joan Baez
18. Chrissie Hynde
19. Laura Branigan
20. Meat Loaf — the picture shows Cher

33 · R · PUNK

1. Johnny Rotten / John Lydon
2. Iggy Pop
3. The Buzzcocks
4. Generation X
5. Bruce Springsteen
6. The Sex Pistols
7. Johnny Rotten / John Lydon
8. Sham 69
9. X-Ray Specs
10. *The Great Rock'n'Roll Swindle*
11. 'God Save The Queen'
12. Pogoing
13. Toyah
14. Malcolm McLaren
15. Sid Vicious
16. Ramone — the Ramones
17. Nancy Spungen — the picture shows Sid Vicious
18. The Clash
19. The Ramones
20. Lou Reed

34 · P · AKA

1. John Lennon
2. Police
3. Prince
4. Limahl
5. *Barbarella* — the picture shows Duran Duran
6. Madonna
7. Boy George
8. The Jacksons
9. Simon and Garfunkel
10. Boy George
11. James Brown
12. Elvis Costello
13. Meat Loaf
14. Safka
15. Dean Martin
16. Cat Stevens
17. Ringo Starr
18. Cliff Richard
19. Olive
20. Donovan

35 · RPM · HITS 6

1. David Soul
2. Christopher Cross
3. Thunderclap Newman
4. Daryl Hall and John Oates
5. The Hollies
6. 'Africa'
7. The Four Tops
8. Joe
9. Bill Wyman
10. The Mindbenders
11. The Yardbirds
12. Cliff Richard
13. Survivor
14. Dionne Warwick
15. Louis Armstrong
16. Sheena Easton
17. Barry White
18. Jim Reeves
19. Eileen
20. Gene Pitney

36 · MW · LIVE AID

1. His knighthood
2. July
3. Jack Nicholson
4. USSR
5. George Michael
6. Philadelphia
7. Phil Collins
8. Teddy Pendergrass
9. David Bowie
10. 17
11. Phil Collins
12. Green
13. Madonna
14. Daryl Hall and John Oates
15. Duran Duran
16. Bob Dylan
17. Ozzy Osbourne
18. Ron Wood and Keith Richard
19. Belgrade
20. Tom Petty and the Heartbreakers

37 · WM · SILLY SONGS

1. 'Cinderella Rockefella'
2. The Singing Nun
3. 'Mony Mony'
4. Police
5. John Lennon and Paul McCartney
6. The Small Faces
7. 'Ding Dong'
8. The Crystals
9. Sweet
10. Benny Hill
11. Bill — in 'My Girl Bill'
12. The Byrds
13. Robin, Kermit's nephew
14. 'Monster Mash'
15. Allan Sherman
16. 'Yummy Yummy Yummy'
17. David Bowie
18. The Bay City Rollers
19. 'The Streak'
20. 'All Night Long' — by Lionel Richie

38 · R · UP FRONT

1. Eric Burdon
2. John Kay of Steppenwolf
3. The Faces — the picture shows Rod Stewart
4. Bruce Springsteen
5. The Blues Band
6. Eric Clapton
7. Jim Morrison
8. Roger Daltrey
9. Led Zeppelin
10. David Bowie — Ziggy Stardust
11. Paul Rodgers
12. Elvis Costello
13. Elvis Presley
14. Paul Young
15. The News
16. Captain Beefheart
17. The Family Stone
18. Ronnie Spector
19. Bread
20. Elkie Brooks and Robert Palmer

39 · R · THE END

1. Elvis Presley
2. Marc Bolan
3. Charles Manson
4. Elvis Presley
5. *The Catcher In The Rye*
6. Sam Cooke
7. Marc Bolan
8. At the Isle of Wight Festival
9. Keith Moon
10. Boy George
11. Elton John
12. A heroin overdose
13. John Bonham
14. In an aircrash
15. Mark Chapman — who shot John Lennon
16. Elvis Presley
17. Brian Jones
18. 'Mama' Cass Elliot
19. The bathroom
20. Dennis Wilson

40 · P · THE EIGHTIES

1. Five — the album was *Thriller*, the artist Michael Jackson
2. Toni Tennille
3. 'Do They Know It's Christmas?'
4. Paul McCartney
5. Yazoo
6. Tears For Fears
7. Three
8. Limahl
9. 'Will you marry me?'
10. Three
11. Paul Young
12. Fun — 'Girls Just Want To Have Fun'
13. 'To Be Or Not To Be'
14. Chaka Khan
15. 'The Reflex'
16. Bryan Adams
17. Billy Idol
18. '(Clock Of The Heart)'
19. Paul Simon
20. 'Girls On Film'

41 · RPM · HITS 7

1. 'Pop Muzik'
2. Bing Crosby
3. Tina Turner
4. Dave Dee, Dozy, Beaky, Mick and Tich
5. Otis Redding
6. Jennifer Rush
7. The Who
8. Julian Lennon
9. 'Telstar'
10. Manhattan Transfer
11. The sand
12. Vincent Price
13. The Walker Brothers
14. 'Nutbush City Limits'
15. 'Paper Roses'
16. 'Pretty Young Thing'
17. Hotel California
18. Kiki Dee
19. '(Oh, What A Night)'
20. 'Mandy' — the picture shows Barry Manilow

42 · MW · CLASSICS AND NOVELTIES

1. 'I'd Like To Teach The World To Sing' — by the New Seekers
2. 'A Whiter Shade Of Pale'
3. *Hill Street Blues*
4. Mozart — the record was 'Rock Me Amadeus'
5. *Jesus Christ Superstar*
6. 'Classical Gas'
7. Rolf Harris
8. The Royal Philharmonic Orchestra
9. *Pictures At An Exhibition*
10. 'Je T'Aime… Moi Non Plus'
11. The Supremes
12. *Rock Follies*
13. 'Amazing Grace'
14. 'Jupiter'
15. John Williams
16. John Williams
17. The Tweets
18. *Ecclesiastes*
19. *Chess*
20. Billy Connolly

43 · WM · IN COLOUR

1. Yellow — the song was 'Mellow Yellow', the singer Donovan
2. Yellow
3. The Equals
4. Blue
5. Brown
6. Red
7. Fleetwood Mac
8. Green
9. Red
10. Blue
11. Blue Sky
12. Black
13. Red
14. Red
15. Silver
16. Yellow
17. 'Lily The Pink'
18. Purple
19. White
20. Blue — the picture shows Roy Orbison

44 · S · THE KING

1. Pink
2. Colonel Thomas Parker
3. 'My Way'
4. *Love Me Tender*
5. A church
6. 'Are You Lonesome Tonight'
7. 'Heartbreak Hotel'
8. Aaron
9. John Lennon
10. One
11. *Jailhouse Rock*
12. Sergeant
13. 'Heartbreak Hotel'
14. Lonely Street
15. *Blue Hawaii*
16. 'Wooden Heart'
17. *King Creole*
18. 'Are You Lonesome Tonight'
19. Jenna Wade
20. Danny Mirror

45 · R · GOSSIP AND EVENTS

1. Jose Feliciano
2. That he was bisexual
3. Michael Jackson
4. Davy Jones
5. Cass Elliot
6. Patti Boyd (Harrison)
7. Jehovah's Witness
8. Tiny Tim
9. John Lennon
10. Brian Jones
11. Rod Stewart
12. David Bowie
13. Dennis Wilson
14. Jerry Hall
15. Boy George
16. Twenty-five per cent
17. Pierre Trudeau
18. Johnny Rotten
19. Jane Asher
20. Amsterdam — the picture shows John and Yoko Lennon

46 · P · SOLO SUCCESS

1. Robin Gibb of the Bee Gees
2. Julio Iglesias
3. Eddie Fisher
4. Debby Boone
5. Gary Numan
6. Abba
7. Sheila E.
8. Sheena Easton
9. Ray Charles
10. Billy Ocean
11. 'You Can't Hurry Love'
12. Perry Como
13. 'Holiday'
14. 'White Christmas'
15. Barbra Streisand
16. Eddy Grant
17. Boris Gardner
18. Howard Jones
19. 'Mickey'
20. Helen Reddy

47 · RPM · HITS 8

1. The Drifters
2. Cher
3. The Carpenters
4. The Rolling Stones
5. The Chairman of the Board
6. Bob Dylan
7. *Born in the USA*
8. Wang Chung
9. 'Lucille'
10. Madonna
11. 'Lipstick On Your Collar'
12. Duran Duran
13. Roxy Music
14. 'Wake Me Up Before You Go Go'
15. Hero
16. Eurythmics
17. Me
18. Dooley Wilson
19. The Thompson Twins
20. 'All Along The Watchtower' — the picture shows Jimi Hendrix

48 · MW · INSTRUMENTAL HITS

1. Meco
2. Mike Oldfield
3. Glenn Miller
4. The Black Forest
5. Zorba
6. 'Rock And Roll (Part 2)' — the picture shows Gary Glitter
7. 'Exodus'
8. On the shore
9. 'Also Sprach Zarathustra'
10. Focus
11. Green
12. 'Albatross'
13. The Dave Brubeck Quartet
14. Scott Joplin
15. James Galway
16. *The Good, The Bad and The Ugly*
17. Barry White
18. The Shadows
19. Average White Band
20. Emerson, Lake and Palmer

49 · WM · BODY TALK

1. 'Muscles' — the picture shows Diana Ross
2. Dire Straits
3. 'Legs'
4. Roxy Music
5. 'Body Talk'
6. Olivia Newton-John
7. Jerry Lee Lewis
8. 'Heart Of Glass'
9. Queen
10. Eyes — 'Doctor My Eyes'
11. Rod Stewart
12. In hand — 'Heart In Hand'
13. Billy Idol
14. Your feet
15. Your finger
16. Kenny Loggins
17. 'If I Said You Had A Beautiful Body Would You Hold It Against Me'
18. Shirley Bassey
19. Your hand
20. Olivia Newton-John

50 · S · IN PERFORMANCE

1. Mick Jagger
2. Pink Floyd
3. Prince
4. Jimi Hendrix
5. Status Quo
6. Alice Cooper
7. The Who
8. P. J. Proby
9. Jim Morrison
10. Elton John
11. Diana Ross
12. Elvis Presley
13. Glen Campbell
14. Wham!
15. David Bowie
16. Yes
17. The Rolling Stones
18. The Osmonds
19. Mick Jagger
20. Aladdin Sane

51 · R · EARLY DAYS

1. The Bluecaps — the picture shows Gene Vincent with three of them
2. '(We're Gonna)'
3. Guy Mitchell
4. 'Wake Up Little Susie'
5. Eddie Cochran
6. Jerry Lee Lewis
7. Duane Eddy
8. Billy Fury
9. Chuck Berry
10. Little Richard
11. Gene Vincent
12. Little Richard
13. Ritchie Valens
14. Tommy Steele
15. Carl Perkins
16. Chuck Berry
17. Cliff Richard
18. The twist
19. Lonnie Donegan
20. Pat Boone

52 · P · JUST A SINGER…

1. Ray Davies
2. Phil Collins
3. Jimmy Somerville
4. Brian Poole
5. Bay City Rollers
6. Holly Johnson
7. Bow Wow Wow
8. Ian Hunter
9. Spandau Ballet
10. Paul Jones
11. Joe Cocker
12. Van Morrison
13. Simon Le Bon
14. Chrissie Hynde
15. Eddy Grant
16. Nana Mouskouri
17. Daryl Hall and John Oates
18. Phil Oakey, of Human League
19. Aretha Franklin
20. Dolly Parton

53 · RPM · HITS 9

1. 'Vienna' — the band is Ultravox
2. The Bee Gees
3. The Undertones
4. Elvis Presley
5. Peter, Paul and Mary
6. T. Rex
7. The Four Seasons
8. Moon Unit Zappa
9. The Nashville Teens
10. Jimmy Page
11. The Young Ones
12. Ringo Starr
13. Billy Joel
14. The Aga Khan
15. Elton John
16. 'These Boots Are Made For Walkin''
17. Ike and Tina Turner
18. Herman's Hermits
19. Leo Sayer
20. 'In The Groove' — the picture shows Madonna

54 · MW · COUNTRY MUSIC

1. Black
2. Nashville
3. Crystal Gayle
4. Rita Coolidge
5. Woody Guthrie
6. A dagger
7. IV
8. Brenda Lee
9. *The Dukes of Hazzard*
10. Dolly Parton
11. Michael Nesmith
12. Loretta Lynn
13. Glen Campbell
14. Johnny Cash
15. Charlie Rich
16. Loretta Lynn
17. Peter, Paul and Mary
18. Loretta Lynn
19. Dolly Parton
20. A country boy — the picture shows John Denver

Photographic Acknowledgements
Photographs courtesy of Pictorial Press. Picture from *Ghostbusters* courtesy of The Kobal Collection

Picture research by Sheila Corr